Contours of Christian Philosophy
C. STEPHEN EVANS, *Series Editor*

EPISTEMOLOGY: The Justification of Belief   *David L. Wolfe*
METAPHYSICS   *William Hasker (available Summer 1983)*
ETHICS   *Arthur Holmes (projected)*
PHILOSOPHY OF RELIGION   *C. Stephen Evans (projected)*

Contours of Christian Philosophy
C. STEPHEN EVANS, *Series Editor*

Epistemology

The Justification of Belief

David L. Wolfe

InterVarsity Press
Downers Grove
Illinois 60515

© 1982 by Inter-Varsity Christian Fellowship of the United States of America

All rights reserved. No part of this book may be reproduced in any form without written permission from InterVarsity Press, Downers Grove, Illinois.

InterVarsity Press is the book-publishing division of Inter-Varsity Christian Fellowship, a student movement active on campus at hundreds of universities, colleges and schools of nursing. For information about local and regional activities, write IVCF, 233 Langdon St., Madison, WI 53703.

Distributed in Canada through InterVarsity Press, 1875 Leslie St., Unit 10, Don Mills, Ontario M3B 2M5, Canada.

All Scripture quotations are from the Revised Standard Version of the Bible, copyrighted 1946, 1952, © 1971, 1973.

ISBN 0-87784-340-6

Printed in the United States of America

Library of Congress Cataloging in Publication Data

Wolfe, David L., 1939-
    Epistemology, the justification of belief.

    (Contours of Christian philosophy)
    Includes bibliographical references.
    1. Knowledge, Theory of (Religion)   2. Religion—
Philosophy.   I. Title.   II. Series.
BL51.W756   1982   121   82-20345
ISBN 0-87784-340-6

17 16 15 14 13 12 11 10 9 8 7 6 5 4 3 2 1
95 94 93 92 91 90 89 88 87 86 85 84 83 82

For my students

GENERAL PREFACE

The Contours of Christian Philosophy series will consist of short introductory-level textbooks in the various fields of philosophy. These books will introduce readers to major problems and alternative ways of dealing with those problems. These books, however, will differ from most in that they will evaluate alternative viewpoints not only with regard to their general strength, but also with regard to their value in the construction of a Christian world and life view. Thus, the books will explore the implications of the various views for Christian theology as well as the implications that Christian convictions might have for the philosophical issues discussed. It is crucial that Christians attain a greater degree of philosophical awareness in order to improve the quality of general scholarship and evangelical theology. My hope is that this series will contribute to that end.

Although the books are intended as examples of Christian scholarship, it is hoped that they will be of value to others as well; these issues should concern all thoughtful persons. The assumption which underlies this hope is that complete neutrality in philosophy is neither possible nor desirable. Philosophical work always reflects a person's deepest commitments. Such commitments, however, do not preclude a genuine striving for critical honesty.

C. Stephen Evans
Series Editor

1. Introductory Considerations   *13*

2. Approaches to Justification   *19*
   Pure Rationalism   *19*
   Immediate Experience   *22*
   Reasoning from Experience   *25*
   Critical Interpretation   *32*
   Relativism   *39*

3. The Problem of Criteria   *43*
   The Notion of "Criteria"   *45*
   Criteria for Truth   *50*
   The Structure of Warrant   *55*
   The Contextual Nature of Testing   *56*
   The Role of Experience   *58*
   The Status of Warranted Beliefs   *64*
   The Problem of Pluralism   *66*

4. Reason and Religious Belief   *71*
   Doubt   *74*
   Criticism and Religious Commitment   *75*
   The Judeo-Christian Attitude toward Testing   *78*
   A Personal Note   *82*

Notes   *85*

Further Reading   *91*

AUTHOR'S PREFACE

The basic outline of this book began to take shape about ten years ago when I agreed to teach a course in religious epistemology at Trinity Evangelical Divinity School. After teaching it several times there, it received a new embodiment at Gordon College as an undergraduate course.

Along the way I have benefited enormously from interaction with my students. It is chiefly them I wish to thank for refinements in the ideas presented here. Space and memory limitations do not permit me to mention all who have given me valuable criticism and suggestions, but I especially wish to express gratitude to Keith Cooper, Galen Johnson, William Luck and Arthur Moen. It was the encouragement of my students, more than anything else, that prompted me to offer these pages for publication. It is, therefore, a book intended for students who are making up their minds about these important issues.

It would have been unthinkable to have tried this without help in innumerable ways from my wife, Jean, who is the model of a loyal critic. Thanks also to C. Stephen Evans for his valuable comments on the penultimate version. Finally, special appreciation to Robin Dublin and her cohorts for adding the typing of this manuscript to their already busy schedules.

I
Introductory
Considerations

*I*n a famous and widely used book Bertrand Russell wrote
In this chapter we have to ask ourselves whether, in any sense at all, there is such a thing as matter. Is there a table which has a certain intrinsic nature, and continues to exist when I am not looking, or is the table merely a product of my imagination, a dream-table in a very prolonged dream? This question is of the greatest importance. For if we cannot be sure of the independent existence of objects, we cannot be sure of the independent existence of other people's bodies, and therefore still less of other people's minds, since we have no grounds for believing in their minds except such as are derived from observing their bodies. Thus if we cannot be sure of the independent existence of objects, we shall be left alone in a desert—it may be that the whole outer world is nothing but a dream, and that we alone exist.[1]

When I was a freshman taking an introductory course in philosophy we were taught to regard "How do I know the physical world exists?" as a very hot issue. This was the traditional way of teaching philosophy, and the textbooks were organized around this sort of question. Our attempts to generate any heat (let alone light) on the problem failed.

Later, as a beginning instructor, I tried in vain to convince new philosophy students that our knowledge of the external world is seriously problematic. My failure to convince them was due, as I now see it, to the following considerations.

Any attempt to call specific cases of knowledge into question presupposes that we already have cases of genuine knowledge to help us recognize error. To call all knowledge into question is to saw off the limb on which you are seated. Students instinctively resisted this kind of intellectual suicide.

I think my students also strongly suspected that they knew there was a real world, even though they could not justify that knowledge claim by any of the techniques that traditional philosophy permitted. I have now come to believe that the weight of wisdom was on the part of the students who refused to abandon their convictions about the world, others and God. Recent work on these issues throws serious doubt on the sort of assumptions made by the older ways of dealing with knowledge, belief and justification.

Epistemology has traditionally been defined as the study of the possibility and nature of knowledge. Additionally, knowledge was seen to have intimate connections with notions such as belief (knowledge was regarded as a kind of belief), justification and truth. These connections have been classically expressed in the formula "Knowledge is justified, true belief." An enormous wave of philosophical literature challenging the old assumptions about these connections has left the intellectual beach strewn with a tangle of ideas about how knowing relates to other notions usually discussed under the topic of epistemology.[2] We are left with the irony that some of epistemology's central questions may need to be framed without reference to the word *knowledge*, in spite of the fact that *epistemology* comes from a Greek word meaning "knowledge" *(epistēmē)*.

With these considerations in mind, I would like to modify an idea of John Pollock, who said, "The fundamental problem of epistemology is to explain what it is that justifies us in making the kinds of knowledge claims that we customarily make."[3] Whether or not the problem of justification is *the* fundamental or central problem of epistemology is probably debatable. Nevertheless, it is one of the very important and interesting issues in epistemology, and it is the one which I will use for organizing our considerations in this book. My way of approaching this problem will involve the consideration of the conditions under which we may be said to be justified in believing something. To put it somewhat differently, How can we provide warrant for the assertions we make?

The importance of this question was appreciated early in the history of philosophy by the ancient Greek philosopher Plato. In one passage he compares an opinion which has no justification to one of the lifelike statues by the sculptor Daedalus which were so realistic they were reputed to walk off their pedestals.[4] An ungrounded belief is easily swayed and abandoned, *even though it might be correct*. Only when we have provided warrant for our beliefs can we avoid changing our minds irrationally or believing irresponsibly.

Suppose I believe that woolly bears, those furry little caterpillars, are capable of predicting the severity of winter by the width of their color bands. This is, in fact, a not uncommon belief in some parts of the country. What are you to make of this rather strange belief? You must not reject it out of hand. After all, stranger things have been true. More to the point, you might ask what grounds I have for my assertion. What would that accomplish? It would help you decide if I had some justification for my belief. Unless I exposed my reasons you could neither help me discover my mistakes nor come to share my way of seeing things. My reasons for believing in woolly bears could become the basis for a dialog in which we would explore the degree to which we might resolve our disagreements. Presumably, woolly bears either are or are not reliable predictors of winter (we might clarify this considerably in our discussion). The degree to which we are justified in our beliefs about this seems to be dependent on examining available reasons.

Only when human beings take seriously the responsibility of providing warrant and when they are sensitive to the objections of others can genuine criticism and honest dialog take place. The same is true of the ability of beliefs to play a role in the shared, public world and the exercise of whatever approximation of objectivity human beings can attain. An attempt to provide warrant is necessary for a belief to be evaluated.

Not just any attempt qualifies as an adequate provision of warrant for a belief. An attempt at justification may produce good reasons, poor reasons or even irrelevant considerations. A careful assessing of evidence may convince one person that a certain toothpaste is beneficial in preventing cavities. This is quite different from the person who believes the same thing on the basis of an animated cartoon or a private hunch. In the latter case the believer may have no grounds that will withstand careful scrutiny, while in the former the believer may have good warrant.

Of course both of these cases are different from that in which a person believes in the effectiveness of the toothpaste in question because the manufacturers of the product have altered his beliefs by a malicious process of electric shocks and chocolate-candy rewards. We intuitively reject an appeal to the conditioning process as warrant of any kind.

It would advance us significantly, then, if we could establish what counts as a justified belief or, better, what counts as warrant for an assertion. In order to attack this matter as economically as possible, I will (1) begin by describing some of the prominent strategies thinkers have proposed for providing warrant; (2) inquire into which of these strategies, if any, is successful in showing how we might justify beliefs; and finally (3) explore how a plausible attempt to provide warrant might be carried out.

While the significance of providing warrant for our assertions must not be minimized, it is well to keep in mind that recent rethinking of the interrelations of knowledge, belief, justification and truth should make us reluctant to assume that assertions must be justified by some sophisticated process in order to count as knowledge. Unless one arbitrarily defines knowledge so stringently as to make its possession virtually impossible,[5] it seems perverse to deny that ordinary people know what they had for breakfast (or that there are other persons or that the world exists). So for the moment let us shelve the question of how warrant relates to knowledge. We will return to it later, and when we do it will be important to reconstruct the relationship in such a way that we may still be said to know the things we do know. One way to think of this for now is to say that while knowing may be one thing, showing why one is justified in making an assertion may be something else.[6] In that sense, this book is more about showing than about knowing.

Surely one of the most important issues that a reasonable person can settle is that of how beliefs are justified. We all know dogmatists who are more concerned about holding their opinions than about investigating their truth. ("My mind is made up, don't confuse me with the facts.") The worst feature of the dogmatists' malady is that if they are mistaken, they will never discover it; they have condemned themselves to perpetual error. Human beings (including myself) sometimes use their beliefs for wish-fulfillment. Too often we believe what we *want* to be true. I think the only antidotes to this are intellectual honesty and clear thinking about how our assertions are warranted.

I am a Christian, and this makes me mightily concerned about the truth of the beliefs on which my commitment is built. If I cannot bring intellectual honesty to bear on my Christian beliefs, then those beliefs are a fraud, for they claim to be true, not just dogmatic. On the other hand, if one can be both Christian and intellectually honest, then Christianity will have a cognitive as well as emotional appeal.

One need not be preoccupied with religious beliefs to benefit from these pages, for I am approaching this epistemological question in its broadest form—the warranting of assertions in general, not just religious ones. Nevertheless, I suspect this will be most helpful to those who are concerned about the conditions under which we may assess the truth or falsity of religious beliefs. Illustrations of attempts to establish religious assertions will be prominent, though other areas in which knowledge claims are made (scientific, common sense, interpersonal) will not be ignored. So, while the concern for religious epistemology is central to my agenda, this remains a book on *epistemology*. My concern with exploring the conditions under which warrant is possible is logically prior to the justification of particular beliefs, whether religious or otherwise. If you are allergic to being preached at, you may proceed without risk.

2

Approaches to Justification

*T*he history of philosophy includes a number of important strategies for providing warrant for assertions. My purpose here is not to give an exhaustive list of all the possible approaches, but to select several general strategies within which the important epistemological positions fall. This will enable me to expose some of the pitfalls which typically plague attempts to give good reasons for beliefs. I will describe each strategy first and then examine it critically before going on to the next.

Pure Rationalism

This first approach has quite an important history. The attractiveness of pure rationalism lies in its claim to provide warrant which is, so to speak, airtight; it promises absolute logical certainty. A formula for this approach is the following. (1) Justification begins with an absolutely certain starting point not dependent on the ambiguities of experience, a set of premises which logically cannot be doubted. (2) These premises are elaborated by steps using a clear, logical technique. (3) If a belief is included in the elaborated system, it is warranted. Of course, if it is contradictory to any of the statements in the logically generated system, one must conclude that it is false.

The classic example of rationalism is the case of René Descartes (A.D. 1596-1650).[1] Descartes was concerned about placing the infant science of mathematical physics on a firm footing. To do this, he felt that he must prove beyond any possible doubt that the real, measurable, physical world exists.

Descartes decided that he would not accept any idea that was in principle possible to doubt. By operating in this assumed attitude of skepticism he hoped to find a foundation for the structure of his proof. He concluded that while the world's existence was questionable (perhaps his senses were deceived by an evil spirit), his own existence was undoubtable. After all, if I doubt my own existence, who is doing the doubting?

"I doubt, therefore I am" became the foundation of Descartes's system of proof. Yet if I reflect for a moment, I realize that doubting is not the only kind of thinking I do. I think that my desk is brown. I may be wrong about this, but I cannot be mistaken about the fact that *I do think it*. Descartes consequently expanded his "absolutely certain" starting point into "I think, therefore I am." To this he added other assertions which he took to be likewise undoubtable, such as "nothing can come from nothing" (that is, all effects have causes) and "a cause must be at least as great as its effect."

From this base of certainty Descartes went on to notice that he had an idea of a Perfect Being (God). This is not in itself any guarantee of the truth of such an idea, but it is undoubtable that I at least *have the idea* of God (like my idea of a brown desk).

How, Descartes inquired, did I come to have such an idea? I did not produce it, because I am imperfect. After all, the idea of a

Perfect Being must have a cause ("nothing comes from nothing"), and its cause must be perfect ("a cause must be at least as great as its effect"). So the cause of this idea must be a Perfect Being itself.

But Descartes did not stop there. He pointed out that if there is a Perfect Being (God), that Being would be perfect in goodness. If that Being were perfect in goodness, then it would not deceive us about the existence of a physical world that (at least in its measurable properties) corresponds to the one reported by our senses. Since there is a Perfect Being, the physical world exists! Descartes had (he was sure) proved there is no evil spirit deceiving us.

Now notice what Descartes has tried to do here. He has attempted to achieve a starting point that is absolutely certain; he has related these undoubtable assertions in logical steps so as to (he hopes) preserve this certainty in all of the later conclusions; finally, in this logically related string of assertions he finds the assertion "the physical world exists" included.

There are some problems with the strategy of pure rationalism that have made most contemporary philosophers quite suspicious of the sort of claims rationalists once made.[2] Genuinely certain starting points are pretty elusive, and those we can find are utterly skimpy. For example, that I now have a headache may be undoubtable to me, but what can I possibly infer on the basis of logic alone from this fact? Actually, most of the candidates for absolute certainty turn out not to be at all certain after closer inspection. Take Descartes' notion that a cause must be at least as great as its effect. This is taken by Descartes to mean that whatever is true of the effect must also be true to the same or greater degree of the cause. Yet counterexamples to this principle abound. In his excellent discussion of the Cartesian argument, Frederick Ferré points out that the beauty of Helen of Troy may have caused the Trojan War, but certainly this does not imply that what is true of that war was also true of her face.[3]

Thus it becomes necessary for the rationalist to smuggle in assumptions from experience, tradition, what is "self-evident" at a given time to a given culture, and so forth. Otherwise the proof never gets off the ground. But since in a logical proof one's confidence in the truth of the conclusion must not exceed one's confidence in the truth of the premises, the claim to airtight demonstration fails. The rationalist has taken an important procedure, deductive logic, and made what turns out to be unrealistic claims for it. Our criticisms should not blind us to the significance of deductive elaboration in mathematics, symbolic logic and as a control in thinking and argument. Nevertheless, the rationalist has not made good the promise of providing proof for beliefs in a way that guarantees freedom from all possible doubt.

If we grant that we are not likely to have absolute logical certainty for our beliefs, if we grant that we shall have to settle for something less airtight, what are some of the options? In the following sections we shall look at three. None of them comes to us with the epistemological optimism that pure rationalism had, but all of them attempt to offer something positive in the way of providing warrant.

Immediate Experience (Naive Empiricism)
Have you ever said, "Seeing is believing"? It is attractive to think that at least some of our experiences present us with information which is, not logically certain—since logic has nothing to do with it really—but at least psychologically certain, undoubtable under any imaginable conditions.

A short formula for this might be the following: (1) Justification consists of a direct awareness of the object or person about which you wish to justify your belief. (2) If the consciousness is really direct, what you are aware of will not only be beyond your own control but your beliefs about it will not be questionable or need to be justified in terms of anything else. This sort of knowing is sometimes called self-authenticating because the experience is regarded as its own warrant. If you have really experienced something (it is claimed) nothing could properly call your beliefs about it into question.

In our unreflective, common-sense attitude we often take our experiences of the world and of others to be self-authenticating in this sense. Nothing could replace the experience of being out in the rain to give you confidence in your belief that it is raining. Many twentieth-century thinkers have seized upon this approach as a way of justifying belief that is more plausible and natural than rationalism. A whole group of thinkers has claimed that our belief in the reality of the physical world is warranted in this way. Jean-Paul Sartre, Martin Buber and others have claimed that our experience of other persons is genuinely of this sort; the intuitionist Henri Bergson has claimed that it is possible to experience directly the inner nature of reality; and a wide variety of religious writers have claimed that religious experience or religious encounter gives us direct warrant for belief in God.[4]

Sometimes, especially in the area of religious experience, it is claimed that the knowledge so gained is not capable of being expressed in language, that language is inherently incapable of capturing it. This latter move is unfortunate. If language fails to apply to the experience, then it would seem that such an experience could not function as a justification for saying one thing rather than another. Neither will it do to claim that, since all who share the same sort of experience know what the others mean by "it," language is unnecessary. If the experience or what is experienced cannot be described, what could it possibly mean to talk about the "same sort" of experience, let alone know what is meant by "it."

Not all of those who appeal to experience go this far. Many claim that what is experienced *can* be described, and that the description is justified by the immediate experience. Let us look into this. Take the claim that our knowledge of others is immediate and self-authenticating. What about the ancient Egyptian who experienced his cat as a personal "other," perhaps even a "divine other"? What about the primitive who experiences plants as "others"? Then there are those who claim that we have immediate experience of the existence of the world of physical objects. But many thinkers have held that it is self-evident that all of our perceptions are private events occurring in the interior of the mind, that physical objects are logical fictions constructed out of such sense experiences.

The realm of religious experience is an even more dramatic confusion. Every religion, primitive or worldwide, has its visions, changed lives and conversions. Each has its representatives who with serene confidence or rabid fervor appeal to their personal experiences which validate their religious claims. The radically different (in many cases incompatible) nature of the accounts strongly suggests that the experiences are not self-interpreting. In fact, the accounts are usually given in whatever interpretive framework is culturally, philosophically or religiously available. What is taken as self-evident seems to be something that the perceiver brings to the experience, at least in some important sense.

As one writer has put it:

Historians and philosophers of science . . . students of language and knowledge . . . as well as students of perception agree that factual statements are conceptually contaminated. . . . How a scientist sees the world is no more a matter of veridical observation, *in any absolute sense,* than is the way a culture-bound person sees the world that is unique to his frame of reference. The welter of pre-perceived events may be factually and theoretically neutral, but just how our events-as-experienced are precipitated from this neutral stuff is a complicated constructural matter involving sensitivity, selectivity, and the entire epistemic apparatus of structuring which is prior to the experience itself.[5]

An appeal to immediacy fails to function as a way of providing warrant for our beliefs *when there is conflict* about what we can claim to have immediately experienced. Even if someone has experienced (or if we all experience) the world, others or God directly, how do we discriminate erroneous, but convincing, experiences from genuine ones? There might be an answer to this, but it is hard to see how a repeated appeal to experience could be that answer. The answer to the question as to whose experience is correct cannot be decided on the basis of experience *alone*.

Undoubtedly we do use experience as our point of departure in most of what we believe, and necessarily so. But experience is not immune to challenge, and what we believe on the basis of experience may need to be revised under certain conditions. Of course, this means that under certain other conditions revision will not be necessary. We clearly need to explore those conditions, but for now the point is that experiences are not infallible or self-authenticating.

Reasoning from Experience (Inferential Empiricism)
Perhaps if we had thought about it a little more before we began we would have realized that human disagreements are too deep-rooted to be resolved by something so simple as an appeal to experience. Sometimes those who admit this think that it is because really important beliefs are about things that we do not experience immediately, whether they be atoms, physical objects, others, God or the past. For these thinkers, science, common sense, theology and history (as well as all other important forms of human thinking) operate by making inferences about what is not experienced on the basis of what is experienced. Sir James Jeans said that the job of physical science is to infer knowledge of physical objects from a set of signals passing along our nerves.

A formula for this strategy might go like this. (1) Justification begins by ascertaining the data actually given in experience. (2) That data is then manipulated using some type of inductive principles. (3) As a consequence of this manipulation, probable facts may be established about that which is beyond our experience (at least our present experience). The inductive principles mentioned in (2) may vary some from discipline to discipline. In history they are the rules of historiography; in science they are the scientific method or the sort of inductive principles usually discussed in the sections of logic books given over to inductive logic. In all of the forms of reasoning (according to the proponents of this approach), there is some set of principles which permits us to establish causal connections or analogies between that which we actually observe and the unobservable affairs for which we are trying to provide warrant.

Let us look at some examples of the ways such a strategy is supposed to work. "Where there's smoke, there's fire," we say. This is an example of such reasoning. Our belief that there is a fire is justified by the presence of smoke; that is, we infer the existence of fire (which we do not see) from the smoke (which we do see), because fire and smoke are causally related. Sometimes science has been supposed to work in this way. Francis Bacon, and later John Stuart Mill, believed that scientific progress need not be dependent on the personality or ingenuity of any given scientist, but that anyone of normal intelligence could make scientific discoveries if only he or she knew the proper procedures.[6] These procedures were formalized into principles of induction which allowed the discovery of causal relations between variables in a routine and mechanical way. The data are manipulated inductively, and causal connections which go beyond our present experience are supposedly established.

For example, imagine that many members of a community fell ill with food poisoning. Suppose further that all who got sick had eaten a certain brand of canned mushrooms (method of agreement), that nobody got sick who had not eaten them (method of difference), and that those who ate the most were the sickest (method of concomitant variation). We might inductively conclude that the canned mushrooms and food poisoning were causally related, even with respect to as yet uneaten cans.

With regard to perception, the sort of view attributed to James Jeans is fairly common in the history of modern philosophy and psychology. According to John Locke, Bertrand Russell and many others, we do not experience the physical world directly; indeed, we cannot experience it directly. Our belief in the existence and nature of the physical world is an inference from what we do know directly, namely sensations, sense data, neurological impulses or the like.[8] We believe that there must be physical objects that cause sensations, so (it is claimed) the inference is a causal one.

Our belief in other minds is supposed to be supported in a similar manner. My conscious experience and thought is intimately related to my body and its behavior. This is the data from which I begin. There are other bodies which resemble my own and which behave like mine. From the similarities (analogies) between those bodies and mine, I conclude that I am warranted in believing that there are, in all probability, conscious experiences associated with those bodies as well.[9]

So also the argument runs with respect to religious knowledge. Data in nature (for example, order in the universe) or history (for instance, fulfilled prophecy, unusual events) are taken as starting data. Causal inferences (usually of an informal sort) are made concerning the sort of cause (usually taken to be a divine Being with appropriate attributes) that is likely to be connected with such data. Sometimes the inferences are made on the basis of an analogy; for example, intelligent design is associated with certain sorts of order. Therefore, similarly the order we observe in the universe must be associated with a superior intelligence.[10]

In all of these examples one begins with an initial set of data and draws conclusions about more remote states of affairs by techniques that allegedly establish some connections between the observed data and those states of affairs not observed. I suppose that all of this has a certain appeal, and in fact an inferential strategy has had much influence in the history of Western thought. Nevertheless, this approach seems to have played itself out and has considerably fewer advocates now than just about any time since the Middle Ages. Part of the reason for this is the dead end to which the Scottish philosopher David Hume (A.D. 1711-1776) took the logic of this approach. Once one subscribes to this strategy, one opens oneself to certain criticisms which appear unanswerable without abandoning the approach altogether. Though not all of the criticisms we are about to examine are Hume's, anyone familiar with Hume's thought will recognize the contribution he has made to exposing the bankruptcy of this approach. In his philosophical works, especially *Treatise of Human Nature,* *Inquiry Concerning Human Understanding* and *Dialogues Concerning Natural Religion,* Hume sought to show that neither the existence of God, the existence of a physical world, cause and effect relations, nor even the existence of the self can be made philosophically plausible. (In spite of this he believed it was humanly necessary to believe in all of these, except the existence of God.)

Our formula for this strategy began with establishing the facts actually given in experience. Are there indeed some neutral data given in experience from which we might begin? There might be, but this is the same problem we encountered in our discussion of immediacy (p. 24). The supposedly neutral objects of our experience may be interpreted in more than one way, perhaps a great many ways. How we interpret depends on the interpretive scheme at hand in our cultural situation. This means that we do not unambiguously read the meaning of an event off the face of experience. We may seem to do so because we see the world through the spectacles of our interpretive framework, but we never seem to be able to claim that we have the uninterpreted facts while someone else is experiencing things in a prejudiced way.

The foregoing is considered by some to be controversial. Suppose for a moment that there were some data upon which everyone agreed, and that these data were susceptible to only one set of descriptions. Even if all of this were granted (though I am not at all convinced of it), the really serious problems of reasoning from experience would be far from solved. The worst problems for this approach lie in the step of *getting* from the data given in experience to the facts beyond experience. Let us look at these difficulties. There are two of them.

First, the facts beyond experience which we are supposedly inferring from the facts of experience often involve information or meaning which goes far beyond the facts of experience. For example, from meter readings and streaks in cloud chambers we infer the existence of subatomic particles; from order in nature we infer the existence of an all-powerful, intelligent deity. But subatomic particles have a multitude of features which meters and cloud chambers do not have, and God is much more than the order of nature (in the minds of those who argue this way). How do we get from the qualities of the things we observe to those quite different qualities which are attributed to the unobserved facts? It is really difficult to see how this question can be answered. The unobserved qualities are not observed *in* the facts of experience, so we don't get them *there* (otherwise we would be back into immediate experience); inductive methods do not add information about experience. They only permit us to make connections within experience or extend our generalizations about experience to future (or all) cases. This really seems to mark a dead end for inductive reasoning from experience.

This very problem has led some philosophers to conclude that we are, in fact, confined to the data of our experience, that no philosophically justified inferences can be drawn. Some philosophers even concluded that physical objects are merely convenient summaries of sense experiences.[11] We might feel like giving up at this point, drawing the dreary conclusion that such skepticism is indeed the condition of humanity. But this will not do. For one thing, in its consistent forms such skepticism rules out any warrant for believing in a public world of shared language. This would not be nearly so telling if those who advance arguments for skepticism did not expect us to understand them. In fact, their belief in our existence should be regarded by them as nothing but a blind prejudice. Furthermore, to permit our search for warrant to be stymied by criticisms directed at "reasoning from experience" is tacitly to assume that the history of philosophy ended with this approach, and that is not so. A number of developments, especially in twentieth-century philosophy of science, make it possible for us to conceive epistemological strategies which we have not yet examined.

The second difficulty with reasoning from experience involves us in a closer look at the nature of inductive argument. Inductive arguments involve the discovery of causal or other relations between two or more variables; for example, establishing the relation between a microorganism and a disease. This permits us to infer the presence of the microorganism when we observe the disease. A little thought, however, reveals the limitations of this type of reasoning. Inductive arguments must be capable of being checked and must apply only within experience, otherwise what we have is just a loose analogy.

Suppose that I were to claim that a particular microorganism were responsible for a certain disease, but that it turned out to be impossible to detect the presence of the organism. Could I use an inductive technique to provide warrant for my belief in the connection between the germ and the illness? Clearly I could not. The success of an inductive argument can only be ascertained after the fact. If I claim that there are functional relationships between two variables (such as germ and illness), the success of my inference from one (illness) to the other (germ) must be checkable. Otherwise we do not know if the inference was successful or not. This means that the application of inductive procedures to areas outside of experience is empty. Only if one has experiential evidence can one affirm that a given effect is therefore the result of a certain cause.

David Hume saw this very well in his criticism of the alleged inference of an Intelligent Designer from the orderliness of the universe. He pointed out that to know that ordered universes are the result of the creative efforts of Intelligent Designers we would have had to observe the creation of several universes.[12] This would enable us to establish inductively the relationship between universes like ours and Intelligent Designers. But, alas, none of us seems to be in a position to fulfill the conditions of inductive knowledge of the production of universes.

Analogy will not help us here either. The reason analogy will not help us to escape the necessity to observe the production of universes is this. An argument from analogy depends on a correspondence between two items, one known and one unknown. For instance, if I were wondering about the durability of my car, I might notice that a number of other cars having the same color had held up well. But this would be a poor argument, because color is not relevant to mechanical reliability. The correspondence between two items must be relevant to the comparison. If two cars are produced in the same year by the same company, then the argument is better because the points of comparison are relevant to the issue of durability. The problem here is that it is only by inductive experience that we know that conditions of production are relevant to durability while color is not.

To return to the subject of universes, we could argue convincingly that the universe had an Intelligent Designer only if we knew that the universe was similar to objects designed by known Intelligent Designers in the relevant (as opposed to accidental or only apparent) respects. But to know this would require an inductive investigation of the conditions which produce universes. Experience is the only way to know that a given effect is really like other effects in *relevant* respects, so that we are justified in believing there to be similar causes.[13] Analogy, in the final analysis, reduces to induction.

The point of this analysis is that inductive inference (despite its admitted usefulness in limited areas) is not capable of carrying us from the known to the unknown. Nothing about the unknown can be said on the basis of the known, simply because it *is* unknown.

Critical Interpretation

There are not many advocates of the previous approach (reasoning from experience) around in philosophical circles anymore (though some persist in other circles, innocent of the problems in their approach). Even basic logic textbooks point out the very limited domain of standard inductive techniques. The reason is not difficult to discover. An inductive approach calls on us to operate without making any assumptions in advance about the outcome of our investigations. It has become increasingly clear, however, that only by making some sort of starting assumptions can the flight to justification get off the ground. The claim that no assumptions are to be made (except methodological ones, of course) is a characteristic of the reasoning from experience approach. Yet, without permitting reason to grow bold and propose conclusions that go *well beyond* the data at hand, we can go *no further* than the data at hand. How might one justify such a flight of imagination?

We have already seen that it is unlikely that we experience anything independent of some set of assumptions. What we see (or otherwise experience) is itself influenced by the framework of beliefs which we use to interpret experience. The logic of the critical interpretation approach is threefold. (1) An interpretation of experience is proposed (at this initial stage without justification). (2) Some sort of tests or criteria are applied to the interpretation. (3) A conclusion is drawn concerning the adequacy or inadequacy of the interpretation. In this approach, warranted belief is a criticized elaboration of one's beginning assumptions. This is likely to sound a bit vague, so we will look at some examples, first from scientific knowledge and then from religious knowledge.

In recent philosophy of science there is virtually unanimous agreement that the older, inductive view of science cannot account for the kind of picture with which science presents us. Using that older approach, talk about subatomic particles, magnetic fields, inertia and the like would never have found its way into science. The construction of theories generally would be prohibited, and only statements about the functional relationships of observable variables would be permitted. Talk about theoretical entities, however, *has* found its way into science. What is going on that makes this possible?

The answer that most current philosophers of science accept is that if scientists do begin with experience, they just barely do so. Very early in the process of scientific thinking there occurs a creative leap of the imagination, what Einstein referred to as an intuition. The mind of the scientist leaps to a possible explanation of the problem with which he is confronted, and hypothesis is born.[14] An example often given of this process is that of Kekulé, the chemist who discovered the molecular structure of benzene.[15] After he had been working on the problem for some time without progress, so the story goes, he was drowsing in front of the fire and in his half-asleep state thought he saw a snake which turned on itself and took its own tail in its mouth. It suddenly dawned on him that the structure of the benzene molecule was a closed ring of carbon atoms. Of course, Kekulé did not run right out and announce to the world that he had just discovered the structure of the benzene molecule in the fireplace! Had he done so he would have become the laughingstock of the chemistry profession, and rightly so. No matter how convinced he might have been that he was on the right track, Kekulé knew that his vision was only the first step in a long process. He had to get the necessary further experience (in this case in the laboratory) to check out his hypothesis.

This brings us to the second step in the logic of critical interpretation, namely, the application of some sort of test to the interpretation which has been proposed. In the presently most widely
accepted picture of science, this takes place in the following fashion. After a hypothesis has been proposed, certain deductions are
made from it; that is, some of its consequences are thought out.
"If this hypothesis is correct, then one would expect to find that
under such-and-such conditions so-and-so would take place."
Situations are set up in which the conditions are indeed fulfilled
and observations are made to ascertain whether or not the consequences take place. If they repeatedly do not take place, we have
drawn a blank. If the consequences do take place, however, then
we are on the road to verifying the hypothesis. Cumulative confirmations of this sort are said to increase the degree of verification or probability of the hypothesis. So we see how this picture
of science fills out the logic of the critical-interpretation approach.
A hypothesis is proposed which is then elaborated in such a way
that its consequences can be tested, and the hypothesis is judged
as having a certain degree of adequacy in the light of empirical
testing as well as certain other tests, such as consistency with already established hypotheses, simplicity and the like.[16]

Some religious thinkers have proposed critical interpretation
as a way of providing warrant for religious beliefs also. In light of
my own concern for clarifying conditions under which such beliefs might be justified, I wish to elaborate a bit here.

As nearly as I can tell, the most sustained, explicit attempt to
apply critical interpretation to religious belief occurs in D. E.
Trueblood's book *Philosophy of Religion*.[17] In this book Trueblood
sets forth belief in God as a theistic hypothesis. This hypothesis is
supported by cumulative evidence which renders the hypothesis
highly probable in Trueblood's opinion. His procedure is to take
various types of human experience (scientific, moral, aesthetic,
historical and religious) and to ask with reference to each kind of
experience, "If theism is true, what would we expect to be the

case in this area of experience?" The designated area of experience is then examined to see if the hypothesis is confirmed or not. This approach is intended to be the same (in principle, at least) as that of the scientist who tests a hypothesis by deducing experimental consequences from it and then carrying out the experiments to see if the hypothesis is verified or falsified.

Trueblood asks, if theism were true, what would we expect to find when we look at the world? Answer: an orderly cosmos of the sort science could investigate. What would we expect to find when we look at moral experience? Answer: agreement among all morally sensitive persons everywhere on the general features of an objective moral order. And so on. Trueblood argues that in each case we do, in fact, find a confirmation of theism. Theism has then, in his opinion, a high degree of confirmation (or verification or probability).

In a similar approach, Edward J. Carnell gives considerable attention to working out the tests of an interpretation (or "presupposition" as he calls it). His conclusion is that the test of a belief is systematic consistency; that is, a systematic fitting of the facts and a consistency with other beliefs known to be true.[18] Carnell argues that Christian theism passes these tests and so is rendered highly probable.

Turning from religious beliefs, it is not hard to see how a case might be made that our common-sense beliefs are warranted in much the same way. We must constantly act on beliefs about matters we cannot check out directly, whether they be physical states of affairs which are presently (or permanently) out of sight, or my wife's loving thoughts, or the reliability of my roommate's character. It might be argued that while I have no direct proof for my beliefs about any of these things, yet some of my beliefs do fit with my ongoing experience and square with other beliefs which I hold to be warranted. So in common sense, too, we have a pattern of an initial disposition in belief (an interpretation) which is tested by how well it stands up in the face of appropriate criteria, and in the process it is granted a certain degree of credibility (or incredibility). Should we not be willing to believe and act on the basis of such tried and true interpretations, these thinkers maintain, not only would all of our theological beliefs be unjustifiable, but also all of our theoretical beliefs in science, beliefs about the past, beliefs about other minds, and, the longer you think about it, beliefs about nearly everything else.

These considerations may make it very tempting to think that our warranted beliefs are, in fact, interpretations which are progressively verified and rendered more probable. There are, however, a couple of dark clouds on the horizon. These are, specifically, the difficulties surrounding the concept of probability (degree of verification), and the difficulties about choosing criteria to test for adequacy.

The contemporary philosopher Karl Popper has pointed out that talk about "degree of verification" or "probability" seems to be problematic. For any hypothesis there are an indefinite (if not infinite) number of test consequences. Think of the simplest example, "I see a physical object before me." The process of verifying that statement involves an (in principle) endless number of possible perceivings of the object, both personal and interpersonal (confirmations of what I see by others). At any point if the harmonious development of the perceptual process goes awry (say, the visual object turns out not to feel solid or others fail to perceive what I perceive), doubt is cast on the belief, no matter how plausible it was initially. The point is that if there are an indefinite number of test instances for a hypothesis, then no mathematical formulation of its probability is possible. (Try dividing a given number of confirming test instances, say twenty-five, by an indefinite number to see what probability you have achieved. Of course, you cannot do it until you know what the indefinite number is, but that is just what we do not know when testing a belief.) If the number of test consequences trailing off into the future are counted as being infinite, then the probability of a hypothesis can never rise above zero.

In a sense all of this is philosophical nitpicking (albeit nitpicking with which many great minds have grappled) alongside the really formidable problem that faces any attempt to talk about the "degree of verification" of a hypothesis. The notion of verification is based upon a logically invalid argument form. When we attempt to verify a hypothesis, we are in effect saying, "If this hypothesis is true, then this consequence follows from it. This consequence is, in fact, the case. Therefore, this hypothesis is true, or at least probable."[19]

Very little reflection is required to see that this argument has the same form as, "If my cat has been stolen, then she has not come home. My cat has not come home. Therefore my cat has been stolen." But this argument works only if I know *in advance* that the *only reason* my cat would not come home is that she was stolen. In fact, although it is true that if my cat has been stolen, she would not come home, it is equally the case that if my cat has been hit by a car, she would not come home. So also if she were lost in the woods, accidentally locked in someone's garage, absorbed in an especially good mouse hunt, having kittens, asleep in the catnip, or perhaps a multitude of other situations undreamed of by human being (or cat). What *can* be said logically about my stolen cat hypothesis is that it is false if my cat has come home.

The logical form of verification is:

$$\frac{\begin{array}{c} p \supset q \\ q \end{array}}{p}$$

(That is, p implies q; q; therefore p.) This is invalid. On the basis of q, nothing at all can be said about p. The fallacy is sufficiently seductive that logicians have seen fit to give it a special name, "affirming the consequent." On the other hand, while a hypothesis cannot be validly verified, it can be falsified. The valid argument form for falsification is as follows. It is called by logicians *modus tollens:*

$$p \supset q$$
$$\sim q$$
$$\overline{}$$
$$\sim p$$

To justify any interpretation by extracting test consequences from it and then affirming them falls into the trap of affirming the consequent. This procedure does not verify the interpretation in question unless you already know that *no other interpretation could possibly account for the positive result.* As in the example with my cat, we almost never know this. The best we can do is to try to eliminate false interpretations (or hypotheses).[20]

This, however, introduces another rub. Even the falsification of an interpretation depends on having criteria (tests) which the hypothesis might violate. There must be a negative set of conditions which falsify the interpretation. How is it possible, then, to get criteria for evaluating an interpretation upon which all the persons interested in it will agree? The criteria must not be arbitrary, and they must be binding upon all who wish to evaluate the belief. This turns out to be a tall order. We might try to show that a given set of criteria was the correct one, but this would seem to involve the difficulty of getting a new set of criteria by which to evaluate the first, and so on *ad infinitum.*

To attempt to justify the criteria by appealing to self-evidence would involve difficulties we have already examined (under immediacy, p. 24). The futility of that would be exposed by having someone else appeal to the self-evidence of another set of criteria. To evaluate the criteria by themselves would be circular; to establish the appropriateness of the criteria by deducing them from the hypothesis to be tested would be question begging.

But wait a moment. Surely anyone would have to admit that a hypothesis must be tested against the facts. This move, however, does not quite turn the trick. Are some facts more important than

others in assessing any hypothesis? Can some facts be safely ignored or put on the back burner for the time being? And then,
as we have already seen, agreement about what the facts are and
what they mean depends (at least in many cases) upon the interpretive framework or hypothesis under which one is working.
The "facts" of psychology do not look the same to a behaviorist
as they do to a humanistic psychologist. This problem has created
some very interesting issues in recent philosophy of science. A
wide spectrum of thinkers agree that how one interprets scientific data depends heavily upon the interpretive framework within
which one is working. As it is sometimes put, "All seeing is
'seeing as.' "[21] That is, seeing something is seeing it *as* a certain
sort of thing that fits in with other things in a certain way. One
must actually *learn* to see things in a certain way, or the relevant
facts remain opaque. The lay person must learn to see like the
physicist, or the streaks across a cloud chamber are apt to be over-
looked as meaningless and certainly will not be seen as paths of
electrically charged particles. Even within science advocates of
rival hypotheses may not be able to agree on what the facts are
because their theoretical predispositions are so different.[22]

In religious matters factual disagreement may be even more
troublesome. Some Christians point to the miracles of Christ as
facts which falsify philosophical naturalism; but philosophical
naturalists do not regard the miracles as a serious challenge because they do not accept them as facts (at least in the sense that
Christians do). The presence of order in the universe is differently
perceived and interpreted by the theist and the naturalist; indeed,
the naturalist may perceive what the theist calls order as merely a
special instance of disorder. As we have seen in several contexts
now, the data of experience is itself problematic and in need of
interpretation.

Relativism
Now we must face where all of this leads. If our beliefs are a web

of interpretations which organize experience, then the possibility of providing warrant for our beliefs depends upon there being appropriate criteria for recognizing adequate interpretations and rejecting inadequate ones. The criticisms of the critical interpretation approach mark the end of the road, unless we can overcome them in some way or find an alternate route to providing warrant. At this point quite a number of recent thinkers have decided that it is wise to throw in the towel. Along the whole gamut of epistemological arenas, some form of relativism has its champions. Scientific hypotheses cannot be decisively falsified according to these thinkers, because facts are already interpreted and what criteria or procedural rules are brought to bear depend upon the prior commitments of the scientists.[23]

Likewise, world views and metaphysical systems are held to be a function of the perspective of an individual or group at a certain time and place. Here as in science it is said that no fruitful dialog can take place between proponents of rival positions because they subscribe to different rules or criteria.[24] It would hardly come as as surprise if relativism were proposed in religious belief. After all, if science is infected, surely religion would not be otherwise. If we lack the ability to offer genuinely (or universally acceptable) rational grounds which justify one view of reality rather than another, then a religious person is one who is *simply* committed to seeing things a certain way. Nothing can threaten this belief, and such a person cannot challenge rival beliefs with any effectiveness. No religious position is refutable, according to this position, though some add that we will find out who was right in the afterlife. (Of course, if there were no afterlife, this would be a falsification of their position, though hardly an informative one.)[25]

Let me try to pull together the threads we have spun to this point. In order to look into this business of providing warrant for our beliefs, we surveyed a broad sampling of attempts to provide justification, both past and current. The result was disappointing and left relativism as a tempting alternative. It seems to me that one fruitful direction to go from here is to face the difficulties with the critical interpretation approach head-on.

Overcoming these difficulties involves swallowing two hard mental lumps. The first lump is a proposal I will make about criteria for evaluating interpretive schemes. If such criteria are not achievable, then relativism is unavoidable and beliefs cannot be warranted. The other lump will be to see warrant itself in a new way. To overcome the problems with verification we will have to take our old view of what a justified belief is and virtually turn it inside out.

3

The Problem
of
Criteria

I do not have it in for relativism. In many respects I find it a fascinating, even attractive, alternative. It engenders epistemological humility, defeats an arrogant pomposity in belief, even promotes a sort of democratic ideal in matters of knowledge. Perhaps its most comforting feature is that it requires no hard work at all in the matter of justifying beliefs.

What makes me uncomfortable about relativism is that it gives me neither motive nor strategy for guarding against self-deception. Like Winnie-the-Pooh, I think I may sometimes be "foolish and deluded" in what I believe. Of course, it may be the case that no belief is any better than any other and that there is no such thing as self-deception, yet I cannot bring myself to agree to that.

Perhaps some beliefs *are* inadequate or even false. I think as a philosopher I would be lying down on the job if I did not try to discover whether there are conditions under which false beliefs might be distinguished from true ones. That is exactly what I am going to attempt in this section. Of course, I would be fooling you if I implied that at this point I do not know how all of this is going to turn out. Obviously by the time you read this I will have long since written (and rewritten) the pages that follow. Nevertheless, I want you to try to think along with me on this inquiry as if we were in actual dialog. Only in this way will you be able to get inside of my thinking enough to help me discover if I am deluded in believing that I have a constructive way of by-passing relativism. Only by doing this will it count if you should end up agreeing with something that I develop. The philosophical enterprise is a critical endeavor, if it is anything.

One warning about what follows. I do not intend to come up with pat answers to the difficulties we posed for the various approaches. I plan to take the difficulties seriously. The implication that personal commitments play an inescapable role will be fully faced, though I will try to show that these subjective elements, which some believe to lead to relativism, do not really do so. What results may be in some respects startling. It may even be a little disconcerting. I believe that the more you think about it, the more you will see that it is not really so outlandish as it appears at first glance and is enormously close to common sense. All of this will come into focus when we have the proposal before us.

An overview of where we stand after our criticisms of the traditional epistemological strategies have settled out seems to be in order.

The prominent American philosopher W. V. O. Quine has given a picture of beliefs that seems to describe pretty well where we have come out. He proposes that we think of our beliefs as forming a complicated, interconnected web of ideas.[1] Some of the beliefs constituting this web lie at the edge of the web, very close to experience; other beliefs lie rather far from experience, more toward the interior of the web, so to speak. Like the inner portions of a physical web, these interior portions of the web are essential to holding the web together. Logically they are part of a global set of beliefs about what reality is like. Let us call this, as I have earlier, an interpretive scheme or framework. It is the integrity of the web of beliefs which gives the inner beliefs their meaning. They have a function in the web which is not simply social or emotional, but cognitive. They are part of an interpretation of reality which seeks to come to terms with experience in a total rather than a piecemeal fashion.

This account of the meaningfulness of beliefs which are not directly related to experience is by no means restricted to religious beliefs. It pretty clearly applies to scientific, common sense and other beliefs as well. If we believe in atoms, the love of a friend, other minds, and the other side of physical objects, we do so not because they are demonstrable on the basis of strict adherence to sense perceptions presently given, but because they are part of a network of beliefs which enables us to orient ourselves to and get around in experience.

The difficulties of assessing such a web of beliefs remains. I will address those difficulties in the following order. (1) How is it possible to gain criteria which are not merely arbitrary in order to appraise interpretive schemes? (2) Closely related to this but separated so it can be explicitly discussed is the question, How can experience be of any help in assessing an interpretive scheme if experience itself is interpreted in light of that scheme? (3) If one cannot gain conclusive verification for an interpretive scheme, what sort of standing is it possible to ascribe to beliefs which are genuinely warranted (assuming that we can get past the first two problems)? The first of three problems will be treated next and will form the context in which to discuss the latter problems.

The Notion of "Criteria"

Under what conditions is it possible to talk about criteria at all? To begin with, suppose someone sets a task for me to do, such as write a term paper for a course. How shall I determine if I have completed the task at all sucessfully? The answer to this is, I think, by attending carefully to the assignment and being as clear as possible about what the professor meant by the terms he or she used in making the assignment. That is the first step. The second step is to take this clear picture of what was expected of me and to compare it with what I actually did. If at the outset I determined that my professor includes in the idea of a term paper that it must be of such and such minimum length and be documented in a certain way, my failure to do these things will cause the professor to regard my attempt as inadequate. If I have clarified for myself the requirements embodied in the assignment, I will be in a position to avoid the embarrassment of presenting an obviously inadequate product; I will know at least some of the criteria by which my work will be criticized.

Or again, suppose that I set a task for myself such as being able to predict lunar eclipses. In order to determine if I have successfully achieved my goal, I will have to clarify for myself exactly what I am trying to accomplish. Unless I am clear about what counts as a lunar eclipse and how accurate a prediction must be to count as a prediction, I would flounder about indefinitely without being able to determine if I had completed what I set out to do, let alone be able to criticize the adequacy of my work. Tasks (or, as I shall call them, projects) are like that. If you have a project, then you have criteria as a result. Criteria are, at least in the cases we have examined, simply a clarification of the project we or someone else sets for us. In such cases the criteria are not arbitrary with respect to the given project, *they are the project*. More precisely, they are the project formulated as a set of standards by which we can test the outcome of attempts to carry out the project.

Granted, there is a sense in which the project itself might be arbitrary. I can take it on or refuse it. But once I take it on, to refuse to have my efforts judged by what the task requires is to abandon the project. In this sense criticism requires commitment to a project. Where there is no such commitment, there seems to be no hope of gaining criteria. What, in fact, could it mean to have criteria which were not related to some project or another? Perhaps there is an answer to that question. Perhaps there could be such a thing as criteria which hang in midair, so to speak. We do not need to know the answer to this in order to proceed. It suffices for our purposes to realize that at least in many clear cases criteria function to assess how adequately we have carried out a project, and that in those cases they are derived by a clarification of the project itself.

So far so good. And not too complicated either. Neither is the next point. Projects may be divided into several distinct kinds. For example, there are projects which are concerned with producing systems of assertions which make sense out of our experience (interpretive assertions). Let us call these *theoretical projects*. Some other projects are mainly concerned with the production of certain behaviors, others with the rearrangement of matter into certain shapes and functions (neither linguistic nor behavioral). These various practical projects could be classified and labelled, if we wished. Other sorts of projects may be concerned primarily with the production of certain experiences and emotions. We might be able to expand this list of possible projects considerably, but this is sufficient to help get the flavor of the variety of types of projects there might be and how they might be classified.

One more observation about projects before we try to pin down the notion of "truth." Within each type, projects vary with respect to degrees of generality; that is, it is possible to arrange a list of projects within each type in order of increasing generality, so that the less general projects are seen as special cases of the more general ones. For example, being able to do a handstand on the parallel bars is less general than having mastered the parallel bars, which is in turn less general than being an accomplished gymnast. So also being a good cook is more general than being a good baker, which is in turn more general than being able to bake good chocolate-chip cookies, and so on. All of these examples come from the realm of practical projects. Now take a few from the realm of theoretical projects. A theory (system of interpretive assertions) which enables one to predict lunar eclipses is less general in its scope than a theory which enables one to predict both lunar *and* solar eclipses. Neither of these theories is as general as one which accounts for the motion of all celestial bodies. Still more general would be a theory which accounts for the motion of all physical bodies, celestial and terrestrial.

If you have been brave enough to come this far, you have earned the right to see that talk about truth and falsity occurs most appropriately in the realm of projects called theoretical. So does talk about existence and nonexistence, reality and illusion. The reason for this, in case you have not already seen it, is that all of these terms ("true," "false," "exists," "does not exist," "real," "illusory") are judgments expressed in (and, in the case of true and false, about) interpretive assertions. The word *true* does have other functions. We speak of a wall being true, of a husband being true to his wife, and so on. While these structural and moral senses of true have some relation to the truth which is ascribed to interpretive assertions, it is the latter which occupies us in the epistemological enterprise.

We have already noticed that within a given type, projects differ with respect to generality. Frederick Ferré has discussed the varying levels of generality involved in making sense of experience using the notion of different levels of ordering.[2] The most concrete ordering of our experience takes the form of *empirical hypotheses,* that is, expectations about regularities in our experience. This makes it possible to anticipate the behavior of features of our environment and so orient ourselves within experience at a functional, practical level.

One can always raise the further question of why the regularities in our experience should be there. In fact, much of the more sophisticated sciences, such as physics, involve the production of interpretive assertions which make sense of empirical regularities.

Ferré calls these higher-level attempts at ordering our experience the order of *limited theories*. Such ordering is not restricted to science. Most of us are not content to observe the constant conjunctions of events in other people's behavior. We try to understand why they act that way when certain circumstances occur. Thus in both science and common sense our conceptual universes become populated with subatomic particles, genetic codes, other people's conscious experiences and intentions, physical objects which we are not now experiencing, and innumerable other explanatory notions.

Ferré makes an important observation about this level of explanation. "What is crucial about the order of limited theories is that the scope of the subject matter is always clearly bounded. No matter how many areas of interest the physicist's model of the molecule may serve ... the model will still remain within a certain subject matter."[3] If one wishes to make sense of the *whole* range of limited theories, one must move to the level of *metaphysical theories*.

This form of ordering attempts to unify the entire range of experience (encompassing both empirical hypotheses and limited theories) by locating them within an all-inclusive conceptual map of reality. This is the most general theoretical project of all, attempting to make sense out of the entire range of experience within a single interpretive framework. The sorts of unifying concepts which are introduced at this level of ordering include such items as matter, substance, spirit, God, and the like. (Ferré goes on to point out that when the ultimate explanatory principles of a metaphysical theory are identified with one's ultimate values, one has elevated a metaphysical theory to a religious position.)

I am not willing to defend Ferré's taxonomy to the final detail. For example, I suspect that the general metaphysical commitments we make are already operating in the way we perceive and select at the empirical level. Yet this general ordering has the logical benefit of pointing out the way in which theoretical projects may be ordered in varying degrees of generality. It also aids us in pinpointing the level of ordering (and hence, the theoretical project) to which the truth of a given explanatory assertion belongs.

It is worth noting that we commonly use the word *true* with respect to the certified products of any of these projects. Thus we may claim to have a true empirical hypothesis, a true limited theory, or a true metaphysical theory. The sort of item we wish to assert the truth about will depend upon which level of ordering we are engaged in.

If we wish to articulate the criteria appropriate to testing a theoretical assertion of a given level, we must first specify the project which that assertion is intended to satisfy. The clarification of the project makes available to us criteria for assessing the outcome of that project. Since theoretical projects involve making sense out of some range of experience, both the particular meaning of making sense (explanation) and the range of experience (level of ordering) must be clarified in order to gain the relevant criteria.

Criteria for Truth

Here is a summary of the argument thus far. If we share a common project, we will also share criteria. This is because clarification of a project provides criteria for all who are committed to that project. Suppose we could clarify the family of projects which we have called theoretical. It appears that by doing this we would gain criteria for assessing the truth-value of interpretive assertions.

If we wish to assess how well we have fulfilled the project of making sense out of variables in our experience, we must clarify the notion of *making sense* that we are employing and specify the scope of the experiences to be included in the enterprise. Likewise, to assess our success in making sense out of the empirical hypotheses formulated to cover regularities among variables, we must clarify what making sense is to mean at this level and once again specify the scope of the empirical hypotheses to be covered.

Furthermore, to move to the next level of ordering experience and formulate a metaphysical theory is to attempt to fulfill a theoretical project of the most general kind. *The most general theoretical project is the production of a system of assertions which makes sense out of total experience.* Its generality transcends the limits of any particular domain of experience, so it is not restricted to making sense only out of experience of physical objects and their movements, but includes aesthetic, moral, historical, personal, interpersonal, religious and whatever other kinds of experiences human beings might have. The most general theoretical project, then, is the weaving of a web of assertions which makes sense out of the whole range of experience without arbitrarily ruling out any of it.

The importance of formulating and testing interpretive schemes of unlimited scope (Keith Yandell calls these "total interpretations"[4]) has been well put by Ferré:

> The conceptual quest for a matrix that is whole rather than fragmented, all-inclusive rather than specialized, seems not only continuous in theoretical motivation with more limited modes of understanding but also traceable on its practical side to compelling life needs. At root, that is, this quest is generated by our very practical needs as conscious agents for oneness in conceptual orientation toward the environment with which we must cope. It is nurtured by the need for inclusiveness in the account of things by which we live—inclusiveness that will forestall our being too seriously misled in our expectations, as too often happens when our conceptual instruments have only partial coverage. It is reinforced by the practical needs of a finite intelligence for economy if order is to be intelligible and of any use to us. And it is reflected in aesthetic preferences for elegance and harmony even in diversity.[5]

Furthermore, as I mentioned earlier, it is plausible to many thinkers that our choices among competing empirical hypotheses and limited theories are already influenced by the categories, perceptual and interpretive predispositions, and judgments about reality fostered by our most inclusive interpretive schemes. Nicholas Wolterstorff proposes the following:

In weighing a theory one always brings along the whole complex of one's beliefs. One does not strip away all but those beliefs functioning as data relative to the theory to be weighed. On the contrary, one remains cloaked in belief—aware of some strands, unaware of most. . . . Everyone who weighs a theory has certain beliefs as to what constitutes an acceptable *sort* of theory on the matter under consideration. We can call these *control* beliefs. They include beliefs about the requisite logical or aesthetic structure of a theory, beliefs about the entities to whose existence a theory may correctly commit us, and the like.[6]

Whether you go as far as Wolterstorff or remain with Ferré's account of the significance of the most general theoretical project, the importance of our most pervasive and extensive webs of belief seems quite clear.

Suppose one undertakes to fulfill the most general theoretical project. What does it involve? Let us first investigate how the expression "make sense out of" would function. Suppose that I were to announce that I was slightly under, but considerably over, six feet tall. You would rightfully complain that my remark did not make sense. Or if I gave you a map which had the points of its compass indicating "N," "E," "E," and "E," you could justly claim that given the meanings of north and east, those indicators did not make any sense. In both of these cases it would be lack of consistency (the presence of contradiction) that created the problem. Part of making sense, or a necessary condition for making sense, is an *internal consistency* among the assertions which we make. I think that a case could be made that if we violate this principle, it becomes impossible to make responsible decisions in assigning truth values to statements, even within the context of symbolic logic.

There is more, however, than consistency to making sense; that is only a negative aspect of the concept. Have you ever been perplexed by the wealth of characters and their multiple names and nicknames in a Russian novel? If after several chapters you were unable to straighten out in your thinking the relationships of the various names to the various characters, you might lament your ability to make sense out of the book. Or if you did not see how a friend's dishonest action related to his usual trustworthy behavior, you might observe that it just did not make sense to you. The positive side of making sense is being able to trace relationships among the components of a complex arrangement. In the case of a system of assertions, it is the relations among the various statements which achieve the unification of the system which we call *coherence*. Without this internal relatedness of the statements to each other, we do not have a single system of assertions at all, but two or more separate sets of assertions arbitrarily placed side by side.

So much for making sense. The consistent and coherent system of assertions also has a set of contents. We are not free (within our commitment to this project) to formulate our system of statements out of thin air; it is directed to the entire range of experience. Obviously we do not have the totality of possible experience available to us; we would have to be omniscient for that to be the case. Nevertheless, the goal is to have a system which is adequate for all possible experience, so we must do the best that we can and make sure that it is adequate for all experience which becomes available. To paraphrase a Gestalt therapist I once heard quoted, the system must be able to "gobble up experience." In both the ideal and the actual senses, the system of statements must be *comprehensive* with respect to experience.

It is easier to get a consistent system than a system which is both consistent and coherent. It is easier to get a system that is both consistent and coherent but directed to only a limited domain of experience, than to get a system that is consistent, coherent and comprehensive with respect to experience. Nevertheless, it is this third set of requirements which emerges from a clarification of the *most general* theoretical project.

The fact that our interpretive schemes apply to experience has led many philosophers to propose a fourth criterion, a kind of concern with experience that the criterion of comprehensiveness does not clearly include. Arthur Holmes points out:

> Philosophy is an attempt to take things as they are and to see them as a whole. The emphasis on "things as they are" suggests an empirical criterion. The philosopher is not interested in speculating on what might have been but is not, nor on what might lie beyond the scope of all possible experience, but in understanding experience as men find it in the lived world. [Alfred North] Whitehead's terms "applicability" and "adequacy" are very apt—applicable to what is and adequate to cover all that is. [Stephen C.] Pepper demands that a world-hypothesis have adequate "precision" and "scope"—precision in application to actual experiences and scope in extending to experience of all kinds. [Ian T.] Ramsey and [Everett W.] Hall speak of the "fit" of a conceptual map and of a category respectively, and this seems to include both that it must fit something and that it must fit it all.[7]

The emphasis on adequacy, precision and fit suggests that two different interpretations may "cover" the same set of data, but that one interpretation may clearly suit the data better than the other. Some interpretations are more *congruent* with experience than others.

If we accept this we will add the criterion of congruity to consistency, coherence and comprehensiveness. While I think this is helpful, it also has some attendant problems. Remember that I have admitted that experiencing is an interpretive process.

What does this do to the notion of congruity or empirical fit? This issue will be given special attention later in the section entitled "The Role of Experience."

To summarize, the criteria which result from a clarification of the most general theoretical project are *consistency* (freedom from contradiction within the interpretive scheme), *coherence* (internal relatedness of the statements within the interpretive scheme), *comprehensiveness* (applicability of the interpretive scheme to all experience), and *congruity* (appropriateness of the interpretive scheme to the experiences it covers).

The Structure of Warrant

There may be other ways of deriving these four criteria; nevertheless, the proposal in the preceding section is an attempt to show one way in which it can be made clear why we use these particular criteria which are important in testing for truth.

On the preceding account, it can be seen that in a sense the subjectivists arc correct in their disapproval of the critical interpretation approach. There *is* an arbitrariness to criteria. However, it is not, as they suggested, in the criteria themselves. Once one is committed to a project, the criteria to which one is subject are no longer a matter of selection, but only of clarification. Yet, the project itself is a matter of selection. If my analysis is correct, and the criteria which govern theoretical reasoning are the result of taking on a certain project, then it does not make sense to ask if there are (at least *theoretical*) reasons for adopting this project. The giving of reasons is possible only in the context of the project. To ask for or give reasons simply reveals that one is already committed to the project.

In any case, we can grant the subjectivist that the project is "ungrounded" without losing any ground. It is simply the case that within the company of those interested in matters of theoretical truth, the criteria are not arbitrary, nor are they necessarily the circular result of already believing in a particular interpretive scheme. Instead they stand in judgment on all interpretive schemes from a quite different logical level; they are criteria for and not contents of belief.

The Contextual Nature of Testing

The contents of belief, that web of statements which we are calling an interpretive scheme, are *not derived from* the criteria. The internal criteria of consistency and coherence and the external control of experience are *applied to* interpretive schemes. From where, then, you may be wondering, does the interpretive scheme come? A fair question, but one to which there is no single answer. Some beliefs are suggested by unusual experiences, some are learned at Mother's knee, some are delivered by tradition or other would-be authorities, some are given in dreams, some are given by intuition. I could extend this list indefinitely. The fact of the matter is that we begin already believing some assertions to be true.

Normally our beliefs come to us in a rather undeveloped form, and we elaborate them and seek to understand their implications as we make them more our own. The important issue epistemologically is whether we are warranted in believing a given scheme. It would be a mistake at this point to rule out beliefs because how we came to hold them can be explained psychologically, sociologically or historically. To do so would be to commit what logicians call the "genetic fallacy." The question of warrant with respect to a given interpretive scheme is answered by a thorough examination of the scheme in the light of the criteria. It is answered by casting one's beliefs on the rock of criticism and by seeing (or showing) how well they fare. By such a process of testing it is possible to show that one is (or discover that one is not) warranted in what may be a subjectively arrived at and personally important belief system.

It is essential to elaborate our beliefs and seek to understand their implications. Just as it is impossible to understand what a belief means without a broader context, so also the testing of a belief can take place only within the context of the system of beliefs to which it belongs.

What does it mean to say, for instance, "God exists"? Until this bare-bones assertion is connected with other assertions about God's relation with people, history, nature, values, beauty and whatever else there is, there is no way to know if the God under discussion is Judeo-Christian, Hindu, Moslem or whatever. Meaning is contextual.

Testing is also contextual. An assertion standing alone cannot be tested. Suppose we wished to test the statement "God exists." The tests at our disposal—consistency, coherence, comprehensiveness, perhaps even congruity—are not applicable to such an isolated statement. A single statement is consistent or inconsistent in relation to one or more other statements. So also with coherence, which is inherently relational. Even concerning the "empirical fit" of our assertions, Quine observes "Our statements about the external world face the tribunal of sense experience not individually but only as a corporate body."[8] Only an interpretive scheme can be consistent, coherent, congruent and comprehensive. An individual assertion can only be evaluated by assessing the interpretive scheme to which it belongs.

There is an important consequence of this. The truth claims of assertions about what really exists can be dealt with only by seeing their relations to a broader interpretive picture of reality which is, broadly speaking, religious or metaphysical. I think this is the case even when the broader context remains tacit or unexpressed. Truth claims always involve at least implicit metaphysical assumptions, even when the one who makes them explicitly denies the possibility of metaphysics. The alternative to explicit metaphysics is not neutrality or no metaphysics, but a naive and unexamined metaphysics. It is not the person who engages in critical metaphysics that is soft minded, but the person who refuses to do so.

The Role of Experience

It is time to face the second issue with which I promised to deal. How can experience be of any help in assessing an interpretive scheme if experience itself is interpreted in light of that scheme? This is a thorny problem indeed. To explore all of the intriguing ramifications of this issue would require technical treatment out of place in a book of this sort, but the importance of the matter will not permit us to ignore it. Our middle road will be to sketch in broad outline how I think it should be approached.

First, a brief summary of the position I am advocating may be helpful. I have rejected all those positions which attempt to justify belief by starting with logical or experientially unshakable beliefs and using those as reasons for holding other beliefs. Any such position which builds a structure of belief on a foundation of undoubtable prior beliefs has been called in recent philo- sophical literature "foundationalism."[9] Instead, I have argued for the view that beliefs are justified by inclusion in a global sys- tem of beliefs that is itself justified by meeting the criteria of con- sistency, coherence, comprehensiveness and congruity.

Next, let us clarify some matters that have stirred up a good bit of controversy in philosophical discussion and are apt to be vex- ing unless we see our way through them. Many issues which have traditionally been labeled *epistemology* are issues which can be settled only after one has adopted an interpretive scheme. This is because they already presuppose a certain metaphysical or ontological view.[10] An example of such an issue is the problem of perception; that is, how does the mind become aware of the world through the sense organs of the body? Providing an answer to this problem presupposes answers to questions about the nature of the world, the body, the mind and the interrelations of these. Clearly it is a concrete epistemological problem, as it already pre- supposes that we have a way to justify our beliefs about the world, the body and the mind. The problem of justification is in a certain sense a prior question.

A number of other issues can be seen in this same way. Questions about the relationship of language to the world (including the much debated issue of how language "refers") will be answered differently by individuals holding divergent interpretive schemes. Clearly how one answers questions about the relations between language and the world (or between statements and the world) will depend on what one makes of the notion *world* and what one thinks about language and language users. (For example, is language a sophisticated instrument of survival in the repertoire of a higher organism in an exclusively physical environment? Is it a means of self-awareness for an all-encompassing, absolute Mind of which individuals are partial embodiments? And so on.)

Then there are questions about the *nature* of truth which some think are primary questions. By now I think you can see how I will approach this. One's *theory about the nature of truth* (but not necessarily criteria for justifying it) is also a function of one's overarching belief system.[11] The options of realism (truth is the correspondence of statements to the world), idealism (truth is the relatedness of ideas to each other; the world is just this web of beliefs), and pragmatism (truth is the property of beliefs which enables us to make predictions about future experiences; the world is the set of presently unquestioned beliefs and incoming experiences) all are laden with metaphysical or ontological commitments. One's theory of truth does not affect one's view of justification of belief nearly so much as the reverse. The all-important question is the warranting of the interpretive scheme out of which we answer these other questions. We can deal with this without settling ontological questions about truth.

In order to avoid being misunderstood on the matter of "concrete" versus "prior" epistemological issues, let me try to clarify their relations. First, our concrete epistemological beliefs are usually temporally prior to what I have called "prior" epistemology. Not only do we have many beliefs which we think are true, matters which we take ourselves to know, but in fact we also make lots of assumptions about how we know and what truth is, all before we do formal philosophical epistemology. If this were not so, attempts to do critical epistemology would never take flight, since they take concrete convictions as their point of departure. Philosophy raises ordinary concerns to a higher level of clarity.

Second, before it is possible to assess a belief system using our criteria, it is necessary to have a belief system on hand. Epistemological criteria cannot operate in a vacuum. The criteria themselves are abstract in the sense of being empty of specific contents. Only when we assess some actual set of beliefs does the interaction of contents and criteria become fruitful.

Finally, in one sense it is also the case that the criteria themselves may be thought of as presupposing a system of beliefs. Do we not, after all, begin with an examination of some things we think we are justified in believing and attempt to abstract from them general criteria for assessing truth claims? I think this is so, but it does not dreadfully disturb the picture I have painted so far. The criteria do not stand *outside* all systems of belief. They are rather trans-systemic in that they are *imbedded* in all systems of belief committed to the project of "making sense out of total experience."[12]

But this does not preclude a responsibility to the criteria on the part of all who are committed to the enterprise, even if it means modifying or abandoning our original set of beliefs. It is *in this sense,* the sense which makes criticism possible, that I mean the criteria represent a "prior" epistemological concern.

So much for this series of clarifications. We now come back to the important issue of the role of experience in testing interpretive schemes. In my earlier remarks I have concurred with the view that experience is already, through and through, inherently interpretive. One's interpretive scheme constitutes the spectacles through which one experiences. How can one test one's theory, if experience is theory-dependent?

Now I think that this is an overly paradoxical way of putting the problem. Surely people sometimes compile experiences which cause them to change their minds. I may have thought that my wife was home when I arrived because of sounds I heard upstairs. I may later fail to find her but discover a banging steam radiator. I change my beliefs. Likewise, a medical researcher may discard a drug in cancer research, although he or she initially had a great deal of confidence in it, because all nonlethal dosages fail to produce remissions.

"Unfair!" I hear the subjectivist object. After all, these are rather low-level beliefs. They are correctable only because the observer has a background of unquestioned beliefs. Quite so, but the claim was that *all* of our beliefs, including even observations, are theory-dependent. What we now have is the claim that, even though our beliefs and observations are theory-dependent, some of them may change. Paul K. Feyerbend, a self-styled "epistemological anarchist," writes:

There is the suspicion that observations which are interpreted in terms of a new theory can no longer be used to refute that theory. The suspicion is allayed by pointing out that the predictions of a theory depend on its postulates, the associated grammatical rules, *as well as* on initial conditions, while the meaning of the primitive notions depends on the postulates (and the associated grammatical rules) only: it is possible to refute a theory by an experience that is entirely interpreted in its terms.[13]

I see no reason why an accumulation of changes might not force quite far-reaching revisions in an interpretive scheme. This could even precipitate a crisis, because far-reaching revisions may produce inconsistency and/or incoherence.

Let me be quite clear, however, about what need not happen in my view. Because our interpretive scheme provides the categories of experience, the context in which we anticipate, the values by which we rank evidence in importance, it is unlikely that a *single* problematic experience would *require* very profound changes in our scheme.[14] Alternative ways of assimilating such experiences will be explored and the one which produces the least change will be adopted. Consider the resistance with which, say, a physicalistic[15] neurophysiologist looks on the results of psychic research. A single striking result would not be apt to change his interpretive scheme. But it is entirely imaginable that an accumulation of results by psychic researchers (perhaps with practical applications) could produce a configuration of experiences which could not be assimilated to the physicalistic interpretive scheme. I am not saying this will happen; it is only an illustration. What it illustrates is the way problematic experiences may accrue to force internal tensions in an interpretive scheme, even though we grant that experience is conceptually contaminated. Where a single, or small number of experiences may be impotent to falsify, a gathering constellation may reveal internal problems.

I think that it can be made clear how this works. Let us return to the imagery of a web of beliefs with the inner parts holding everything together while the outer edge borders on experience. If the scheme is at all well constructed, most experience will be assimilated into its borders without incident. Some experiences, however, may be problematic. The adherent to the scheme may not know what he is seeing; he may see something but not be able to describe it aptly in terms of his framework. One thinks of primitives encountering advanced technology for the first time. A primitive person transported abruptly to Times Square would have considerable difficulty describing what he saw with any clarity. One is reminded also of the visions in the biblical book of Revelation, or the experiences depicted in the science-fiction film *Close Encounters*. For years persons who received radio broadcasts audible only to themselves through fillings in their teeth were thought to be emotionally unstable and prone to hearing voices.

A person unable to deal fruitfully with an experience is faced with several options. Ignore the troubling experience and hope it goes away (regard it as of no importance). Classify it as illusory (merely subjective)—every experiencer does this with some experiences that will not fit in. Take it seriously and attempt to modify the interpretive scheme so as to make sense of the experience. In the interests of cognitive economy, however, the experiencer will probably resist the last move unless the new set of experiences threatens to appear as meaningful for a rival framework.[16]

If and when problematic experience forces revisions in the web, there is no necessity that the web be changed one way rather than another. Presumably some portion of the beliefs could always be preserved intact. (Witness the continued existence of the Flat Earth Society.) The crucial question is, however, "Have the revisions changed the internal structure of the web so that it now violates the criteria of consistency and/or coherence?" We see, then, that even though experience is interpretive (or theory-laden), it may still play a role in the assessment of interpretive schemes.

The role of the congruity and comprehensiveness criteria is to form an important control on the integrity of a scheme. The significance of the congruity criterion becomes clearer here. Part of what gives experience its "bite" in forcing revisions in interpretive schemes is its resistance to unlimited interpretations. Experience may be shaped in several directions, but it is not infinitely plastic, and some constructions plainly do not fit.

Let me conclude this phase of our discussion with the following point. To reject foundationalism is to deny that any particular experience is immune from revision. But *to say that any experience could be revised must be to say that other experiences could accrue which would change our assessment of that experience.* In other words, to espouse an interpretive, contextual view of experience does not prohibit, but makes possible, the reassessment of experience and belief in the light of further experience.

The Status of Warranted Beliefs

We now come to a most intriguing business. It is intriguing because I think it is now possible for us to see that most of the con-
ceptions of warrant with which we have lived in Western intellectual history are wrong-headed. Generally we have sought to
prove that our beliefs are true, or at least show that they are veri-
fiable. When we discussed deductive rationalism we saw the
counterarguments to that sort of proof. When we discussed the
other approaches, and especially the critical interpretation approach, we saw the counterarguments to verification. What then
is left? The cheap answer to this question is skepticism, but this
answer presumes that no reconception of the process of justification is possible. I think that it is.

Suppose you find yourself in the midst of a manifold of experiences (as indeed you do). In order to achieve some sort of
orientation to this situation, you seek to make sense out of it;
you seek to formulate a comprehensive interpretive scheme
which will illuminate your experience, making use of some of
the conflicting clues you find at hand. Can you *prove* that you are
right in your interpretation? I think not. Further examination of
your interpretive scheme from within or in the light of further
experience may show you that you were mistaken. The scheme
may run afoul of the criteria. The application of the criteria to an
interpretive scheme may result in its elimination or falsification,
but it cannot result in final verification.

This is, I think, a consequence of our extremely limited nature
as human beings. But note well. Suppose the interpretive scheme
you came up with *was* true in a final sense; that is, suppose further
experience would never falsify it, and its internal consistency and
coherence were impeccable. It would be the same comprehensive interpretation of reality that an omniscient being (supposing
there were one) would have. The important question from an
epistemological point of view is, however, How could you
show that you had the truth? What warrant could you produce

for your beliefs? To put it another way, What credentials could a true scheme provide to help limited beings recognize it? The only credentials such a true scheme could provide would be its ability to withstand continued criticism. The best in human knowledge consists in interpretive schemes which have withstood strong criticism.

This reconception of the knowing process suggests an answer to the question of warrant with which we started this inquiry. One is warranted, insofar as any warrant is possible, in believing that an interpretive scheme is true provided that it withstands the criticism to which it continually remains open. Let us call such a scheme *corroborated*,[17] though we might also call it *plausible* or even *probable* (in a nonmathematical sense).

Only to the extent that a scheme remains open to continued testing is it able to display its credentials. Only then can it show the strength of its internal structure and its ability to illuminate experience. Far from being a favor, to protect one's interpretive scheme from criticism is to rob it of the only way it can display its claims to truth. I mention this because it is sometimes considered a virtue to insulate one's scheme from criticism. Some Christians, some Communists and some Freudians, among others, share this view. The criticism of opponents are effectively neutralized by appeals to sinful unbelief, class membership or subconscious resistance, all of which make it unnecessary to take the arguments of critics seriously. This may neutralize the opposition, but it also trivializes the truth claims of the protected position. Criticisms must be faced squarely, provided they represent a genuine claim that we have violated one of the criteria.[18]

The strategy for providing warrant, then, is to start where you are. Extend your most important beliefs into a broader interpretive scheme. This may involve a certain amount of self-examination in order to see what your unstated assumptions and their implications are. It may also involve some intellectual house cleaning as you discover inconsistencies and other difficulties in your beliefs. When this is done, you may begin the indefinite procedure of criticism and refinement that is the warranting process. If your scheme is inadequate, the only honest thing to do is to dump it or overhaul it drastically. The discovery of error is a genuine advance, not a loss of face, for the person who is concerned with truth.

If your beliefs are corroborated, you are warranted in continuing to believe that they are true. You might even say in a sense (the sense of "the proof of the pudding"; that is, the test of the pudding) that your beliefs have been proved—but not finally, of course. You may say that you are "sure" or "certain" of your beliefs in the quite ordinary sense that we say we are sure of something when there is no available contrary evidence. We are not claiming that it is beyond any possible logical contest. And you may claim to "know" that your belief is true in the sense that "knowing" (as opposed to simply "believing") appeals to whatever warrant is available and recommends the beliefs to others.

The Problem of Pluralism
There is a temptation to look around at other people who are engaged in the same process. Do not fight the temptation. This is not only permissible; it is indispensable. The first thing that will strike you, if you do this, is that there may be several others who are claiming that their schemes are also corroborated, and that these allegedly corroborated schemes are far from identical. They may even be incompatible. What are we to make of this? Well, would it not be somewhat surprising if, in this complex welter of experience, there were not several apparently adequate ways of interpreting it provisionally at a given time? In fact, there are a couple of important reasons why, apart from incomplete data, the testing process may not *immediately* eliminate an inadequate belief.

In the first place, the coherence criterion is rarely decisive. What it may show is that the scheme is not yet sufficiently elaborated to display all of its inner connections. Of course, if a scheme has been given a reasonable chance over reasonable time and still remains incoherent, it would seem appropriate to abandon it. However, what seems a reasonable chance and time to one person might not seem reasonable to another. There does not seem to be a way of arbitrating the difference between abandoning a scheme prematurely and holding it tenaciously long after it has "gone to seed." Some schemes are inherently incoherent; the pieces cannot be put together, though to demonstrate this in a given case may be very difficult.

In the second place, as we saw earlier, the comprehensiveness and congruity criteria rarely work as straightforward checks against experience. Perhaps there are times when "the facts" count so clearly and strongly against a scheme, or it is so obvious to all concerned that they cannot be assimilated by it, that there is a straight-out empirical falsification. This rarely happens, even in the reputedly empirical enterprise of science. More often the experiences are interpreted in light of the scheme and absorbed into it forthwith, or modifications of the scheme make assimilation of the events painless. As we have seen, some thinkers hold that empirical falsification of a scheme is all but impossible.

Without ruling out the possibility that there can be genuine empirical falsification, I have suggested that the comprehensiveness criterion can have an important function even if the subjectivist is correct about the inconclusiveness of appeal to experience. In order to adjust it to experience, there will be modifications of the internal structure of a scheme. Some additional concepts or rearrangement of existing concepts will be required. This will eventually have the effect of producing internal problems in an inadequate scheme, effects which can be detected by the applications of the criteria of consistency and coherence. Experience, then, is more of a control on the honesty of a scheme than an area for outright falsification. Honest observance of congruity and comprehensiveness produce internal stress which may eventually be fatal, even if the relativists are correct about experiential tests (though they may not be entirely so).

Outright rejection of new data is possible, of course, but anyone genuinely committed to the project of making sense out of experience will be hesitant to do this. It looks like an abandoning of rationality and an attempt to preserve the belief at all costs. This would be to hold one's opinions dear regardless of their truth. Other more subtle attempts to rule out portions of experience, such as wholesale appeal to the notion of illusion, must be regarded as equally suspicious. These are some of the reasons why agreement on the adequacy of interpretive schemes may be delayed. Assessment is complex but not impossible.[19]

Given that at a particular time more than one interpretive scheme may *appear* adequate, I would like to suggest a strategy for this situation. Start where you are. Continue with (or choose, depending on where you are) the interpretive scheme which is personally most important or interesting to you and pursue it as long as it does not succumb to active criticism. There is a genuinely subjective element here. Why not go with the scheme that seems to you to offer the richest view, the greatest hope, the most powerful values? Why not search out the warrant of a subjectively interesting and momentous interpretive scheme before going on to less interesting ones? And if it withstands criticism, it could be profoundly important.

It is clear that one cannot criticize in equal detail all competing interpretive schemes. To criticize an alternative adequately one must elaborate it, extend its application to ever-expanding areas of experience and attempt to live it. By entering into dialog with those who have chosen to test other, different schemes, you can benefit from their criticisms of your scheme and they from yours. This creates optimum conditions to discover your own inadequacies, and if you are onto the truth, it creates optimum conditions to share it with others in the context of their discovery of the inadequacies of their own schemes. Is this strategy of critical dialog incompatible with a genuine conviction that your view is true? Not at all! Surely it is the one who fears he is wrong who avoids criticism. The one who is sure he is right invites it. It only illuminates the strength of beliefs and makes them more available to others.

4
Reason and Religious Belief

I think that now we have an answer to the very old problem of faith and reason. These are not opposites but complementary aspects of the warranting process. Faith is the courage to commit oneself to beliefs in the face of human finitude. As we shall see, only by doing so can reason operate. The believer is a critical adventurer, taking rationally responsible risks. If he or she takes a leap of faith, it should be a leap conditioned by criticism in its choice of alternatives and responsible for continued criticism after the leap. This is the case whether the interpretive scheme to which a person is committed is "religious" or not. The warranting process is the same for the Christian and the naturalist. Both involve the same interplay of faith and reason. Faith in this sense is not the private property of the religious person. Indeed the attempt to test for truth, given that it will eventually involve the wider context of beliefs and assumptions, turns out to be an essentially religious enterprise.

The crucial criticism of a belief system is not whether it involves faith, but if it can survive testing.

In ordinary life there are many areas that make the interdependency of faith and criticism clear. For example, a young child discerns that her mother loves her. This is really a complex configuration of beliefs (mostly unclarified in the child's own thinking) that govern the child's actions and expectations. Sometimes the mother's behavior may seem incompatible with the belief system and lead to doubt. ("She doesn't love me anymore.") However, these minor crises of faith are usually absorbed into a maturing grasp of the mother's actions, and in the long run apparent falsifications are interpreted in a broader context as discipline, mistaken efforts at consistency, personal depression and so forth, which do not reflect negatively on the genuineness of the mother's commitment. Nevertheless, persistent conditions *might* arise which would indeed be more coherent with the belief that her mother did not love her.

In common sense we operate on the basis of beliefs until by so operating we turn up an increasingly coherent set of experiences that challenges or threatens to replace the original beliefs. This applies to all kinds of common-sense beliefs, such as "I can trust my roommate," "You can get a terrific lunch at Hunter's Inn," "This chair will hold me," and so on. If no such challenging experiences occur, then we are warranted in continuing to believe.

In science, too, the interdependency of faith and reason plays an important role. Scientists do not objectively "read" the meaning of natural phenomena off of the world in some impersonal, objective fashion. Scientific theories are risky conjectures that attempt to pull diverse events into a unified account, often proposing the existence of processes and states of affairs which we could never observe directly.

Suppose a physicist notices that some meters are behaving in a slightly erratic fashion. Suppose further that something seems to be messing up the expected results in the cloud chamber or other piece of apparatus. At first the physicist may regard all this as merely an irritation, an interruption of regular work. She or he may, however, come to discern connections among the various irregularities and propose that the presence of a previously unsuspected particle could account for (conceptually unify) the various phenomena. Of course, the disposition to see the phenomena in this way may turn out to be disappointed. In science, unlike common sense, we *deliberately* set out to try to disprove our hypotheses, even though the conditions of *decisive* falsification may be difficult (or impossible) to fulfill.

Science thus proceeds by the collaboration of creative risk and criticism (or as Sir Karl Popper puts it, of conjectures and refutations).[1] Warrant in science consists of continuing to accept into the body of scientific theory those hypotheses which are effective in organizing a body of data and which are coherent with other such hypotheses, as long as there exists no body of counterevidence.

Likewise, the religious believer is one who discerns the presence and action of God in the processes of nature ("The heavens are telling the glory of God" [Ps 19:1]) and the events of history ("And he made from one every nation of men to live on all the face of the earth, having determined allotted periods and the boundaries of their habitation" [Acts 17:26]), as well as in his own life.

As in everyday beliefs, or in science, the believer's faith begins with certain experiences which are "seen" in a certain way (employing a religious interpretation). Alvin Plantinga has argued that just as certain beliefs grounded in experience are basic to our convictions about the world, other persons and the past, so beliefs grounded in experiences of divine disapproval, forgiveness, goodness, presence and so on, are properly basic to our beliefs about God.[2]

As long as the web of metaphysical-religious beliefs continues to absorb and illuminate experience without conceptual or empirical difficulties, it meets the conditions of warrant described earlier in our analysis. Failure to meet those conditions, however, may call the interpretive system into question. So if believers find they cannot explain how the existence of a benevolent, all-powerful, all-knowing God is compatible with the presence of evil and suffering, they may find themselves in philosophical distress.

Religious belief is warranted as a way of making sense out of experience as long as no coherent body of counterexperience arises which cannot be absorbed into the original web of beliefs. In the absence of such apparent difficulties, the religious believer is entitled to the same certainty of conviction that human beings embrace in other areas of belief.

Faith is the creative discernment of meaning.[3] It is also commitment to action on the basis of that meaning, without epistemological guarantees. In these senses it is not peculiar to metaphysical and religious interpretive schemes. It may well be that all human cognitive activity involves the interplay of faith and reason, of insight and testing, of commitment and criticism. This seems to be the case whether one is reading a message, understanding a joke, making judgments about pulling a car into traffic, doing scientific research, evaluating metaphysical systems, or drawing conclusions about the meaning of life. If finite human beings are to have warrant for their beliefs, they must be willing to begin with what they seem to know, seek to eliminate error, take reasonable cognitive risks, and entertain a firm hope of attaining truth.

Doubt

It is possible from this vantage point to assess the nature of doubt, at least in its epistemological dimension (excluding, for example, pathological emotional depression). A believer may be thrown into a state of doubt when suspicions arise that there is (1) some conceptual problem inherent in the web of beliefs, (2) some experiences inadequately explained or illuminated by the web of beliefs, or (3) some rival web of beliefs appearing significantly less problematic or more fruitful. On this last point more needs to be said.

Sometimes criticisms are leveled against an interpretive scheme which have force only if one assumes that the whole position of the critic is true. This happens, for example, when a materialist criticizes a Christian for believing in spiritual realities, or the Christian criticizes the philosophical naturalist for holding beliefs that are contrary to the Bible. In those cases the criticism has force only if one already holds the belief system of the critic. The faith of the naturalist should not be shaken by the claim that she is unbiblical, nor should the Christian be thrown into doubt by the fact that he violates the central tenets of materialism. Only if the critic's position, upon evaluation, appears more adequate than the scheme being criticized will doubt be justified.

When the religious believer finds himself or herself preoccupied by doubt, he or she would do well to specify as carefully as possible the exact nature of the worrisome cognitive objections. Often what mistakenly passes for philosophical doubt is really lack of sleep, lack of social support for one's belief system[4], uncritically identifying with a character in a work of fiction, or some other condition not strictly relevant to issues of truth or falsity. Works of fiction often reflect a definite interpretation of the world, and the reader is led to "experience" the fictional world in terms of that interpretation. If you have read Camus's novel *The Stranger,* you probably have noticed the jolt of switching from the novel to your usual way of looking at things. Such dislocations may induce a feeling of alienation from your previous commitments and may be mistaken for genuinely philosophical doubt.[5]

Criticism and Religious Commitment

Put in the simplest terms, warrant is a process of criticism. Belief systems which survive criticism are warranted; those that do not survive are not warranted. This raises the old issue of faith and reason in a new way: Is religious commitment compatible with criticism?

The bottom line in this question is whether religious conviction could ever be compatible with admitting that conditions are imaginable which, if fulfilled, would falsify that conviction. I believe it is, and to illustrate this compatibility let me take an example from a different area.

I am deeply committed to the belief that my wife loves me. (Incidentally, this is a pretty good example of the way our faith in beliefs is intimately related to our faith in persons, as faith in religious beliefs is related to personal faith in God.) This belief or set of interrelated beliefs influences my way of experiencing the world and provides a kind of background for my self-confidence, emotional security and life purposes. Specifically, it governs my perceptions of her and interactions with her. To abandon this conviction would be to dramatically alter my present perceptions, hopes, expectations and self-concept.

Under these circumstances, could I admit that there are conditions imaginable which, if fulfilled, would force me to abandon this important belief? The answer is certainly affirmative, and I think an affirmative answer to this question is very important. If it were logically impossible for my belief in my wife's love to be falsified under any conditions whatsoever, then there would be no way for me to determine if she really did love me or if I were fooling myself. A genuine conviction that she really does love me is dependent on the possibility of criticism of that conviction.

It is certainly imaginable that a coherent set of experiences might arise which would throw my belief into doubt. The importance of my initial conviction would certainly make me look at this counterevidence *very* carefully before I abandoned my belief. Nevertheless, such conditions *are* imaginable.

Does this mean I am somehow less convinced of my wife's love? It certainly does not. To admit that I would know how to recognize that my wife did not love me is by no means to say that she does not. I would know how to recognize an elephant standing on my dining room table, but that does not mean I believe there is one there! To say that a belief could be recognized to be false does not call any actual convictions into question.

In a very similar way a firm religious conviction is compatible with admitting that falsifying conditions arc imaginable. To say that it is logically possible that my belief is in error is vastly different from saying that I do indeed think it is erroneous. If the existence of suffering could be shown to be logically incompatible with the character of God, then the believer would have to deny the existence of suffering or modify the conception of God's character. The reason this admission does not threaten belief is that it has not been shown that the existence of suffering is in fact incompatible with the belief that God is loving, omniscient and omnipotent.

This willingness to conceptualize conditions of effective criticism is not the whole story, however. It is one thing to note that *if* certain things were the case, then I would be wrong. It is quite another matter to pursue actively the criticism of one's beliefs. Is *active* criticism of religious beliefs compatible with firm religious conviction?

Before I answer this directly, let me recall a point mentioned in passing earlier. In science, it is our epistemological obligation self-consciously to attempt to falsify our theories. This, indeed, is a major preoccupation of science. In common sense the situation is somewhat different. Because our functioning in the everyday social world is so dependent on our common-sense beliefs, we cannot afford the luxury of endless questioning.[6] Time and energy must go into functioning rather than explicit criticism. As David Hume observed long ago, endless unmotivated questioning of the possible nutritional qualities of bread would result in starvation. Yet our very commitment to acting on everyday beliefs does create conditions in which we could discover their inadequacy. If bread ceased to be nutritious, our commitment to eating it for nourishment would place us in an advantageous (but hungry) position for discovering our error.

I think that the criticism of religious belief is much like the criticism of everyday belief. The intimate way in which religious belief functions in everyday living for the genuinely religious person makes it disruptive for the believer to suspend belief for the sake of criticism. Furthermore, religious commitment is more like commitment to a person. In this sense it is parallel once again to my commitment to my wife. It would be inappropriate for me to suspend my belief in my wife's love in order to criticize it. Such assessment must consist of living out my beliefs. But such commitment does put us in a position to detect problems that an uncommitted person might miss. Commitment need not be incompatible with this sort of critical process. So in religious belief, commitment is likewise compatible with criticism. In this case (like the case of everyday beliefs) our very commitment becomes a condition of criticism.

As we attempt to use our religious-metaphysical categories to unify ever broader ranges of experience, we demonstrate their strength or discover their weaknesses. This unambiguous involvement in the critical process is perfectly compatible with a firm commitment to the truth of our beliefs. Fear of criticism is more apt to be related to fear of being wrong than confidence that your beliefs are true. The genuine believer wants to show the truth of his beliefs, and this can only be done in the process of testing.

The Judeo-Christian Attitude toward Testing
I have tried to show that religious faith (discernment and commitment) is fully compatible with the epistemological necessity of criticism. Nevertheless, a specifically Christian believer might be concerned about the way my general considerations relate to the actual attitudes of the prophets, Christ and the apostles in this matter of criticism and faith.

Let us begin by looking at an example of the way in which Jesus reasoned when faced by those who interpreted his ministry and actions in a hostile way. Look at the following passage from Matthew 12:22-28:

Then a blind and dumb demoniac was brought to him, and he healed him, so that the dumb man spoke and saw. And all the people were amazed, and said, "Can this be the Son of David?" But when the Pharisees heard it they said, "It is only by Beelzebul, the prince of demons, that this man casts out demons." Knowing their thoughts, he said to them, "Every kingdom divided against itself is laid waste, and no city or house divided against itself will stand; and if Satan casts out Satan, he is divided against himself; how then will his kingdom stand? And if I cast out demons by Beelzebul, by whom do your sons cast them out? Therefore they shall be your judges. But if it is by the Spirit of God that I cast out demons, then the kingdom of God has come upon you."

This account is imbedded in a series of confrontations between Jesus and the Pharisees. The Pharisees interpret Jesus' healing to be an act of Satanic power. Jesus' response is to show them that if they account for the casting out of demons by postulating the power of Satan, then they must consistently hold that their own disciples are also serving Satan. The Pharisees must make a choice. Either their own disciples were using Satanic power, or Jesus was employing the power of God.

Notice three important things about this exchange. First, the experiential data was not in itself decisive; it could be interpreted several ways. Second, Jesus brought the criterion of consistency to bear on the Pharisees' interpretive scheme; he showed that some of the assumptions which made up their scheme were logically incompatible if elaborated. Third, it was still possible for them to avoid his claim to be God's agent, but only by radically revising portions of their belief system to which they were strongly attached. In short, Jesus did not hesitate to employ the criteria of criticism in exchanges with his opponents.

Paul's argument in 1 Corinthians 15:12-20 is also instructive: Now if Christ is preached as raised from the dead, how can some of you say that there is no resurrection of the dead? But if there is no resurrection of the dead, then Christ has not been raised; if Christ has not been raised, then our preaching is in vain and your faith is in vain. We are even found to be misrepresenting God, because we testified of God that he raised Christ, whom he did not raise if it is true that the dead are not raised. For if the dead are not raised, then Christ has not been raised. If Christ has not been raised, your faith is futile and you are still in your sins. Then those also who have fallen asleep in Christ have perished. If for this life only we have hoped in Christ, we are of all men most to be pitied.

But in fact Christ has been raised from the dead, the first fruits of those who have fallen asleep.

In this passage Paul does two important things. First, he appeals to the criterion of consistency to criticize a belief system. Certain people in Corinth were evidently denying the possibility of the resurrection of believers from the dead. Paul points out that a blanket denial of the possibility of resurrection entails the denial of Christ's resurrection also. These people must choose between two options: either the dead can rise or Christ did not rise (and Christianity is false). The principle of consistency will not permit them to have it both ways. The second epistemologically significant feature of this is Paul's evident willingness to specify a condition which, if fulfilled, would falsify the Christian belief system. "If Christ has not been raised, your faith is futile." Paul's writings are full of attempts to show the adequacy of Christian belief and to raise questions about the adequacy of rival systems. Paul can unreservedly say, "Test everything; hold fast what is good" (1 Thess 5:21).

As a final example let us examine Deuteronomy 18, in which the issue of recognizing genuine prophets is addressed:

I [God] will raise up for them a prophet like you [Moses] from
among their brethren; and I will put my words in his mouth,
and he shall speak to them all that I command him. . . . But the
prophet who presumes to speak a word in my name which I
have not commanded him to speak, . . . that same prophet
shall die. And if you say in your heart, "How may we know the
word which the LORD has not spoken?"—when a prophet
speaks in the name of the LORD, if the word does not come to
pass or come true, that is a word which the LORD has not spoken; the prophet has spoken it presumptuously, you need not
be afraid of him. (vv. 18, 20-22)
There are three things to notice in this passage. First of all, we
actually have here a critical attitude toward what claims to be
revelation. Not just anyone could get away with standing up and
speaking for God. Specific constraints are imposed upon the
would-be prophet so we can discriminate between real and phony
ones. Second, the prophet must relate his message to the Mosaic
teaching ("a prophet like you") and relate his teaching to the
already established words of Jehovah ("when a prophet speaks in
the name of the LORD"). This is an application of the coherence
criterion. A prophet who delivered teachings totally unrelated to
the prophetic tradition was not to be taken seriously. Finally,
then there is an application of experiential or empirical constraints. No prophet whose predictions fail is to be believed on
other matters.

Edward John Carnell has put the biblical attitude about critical
assessment this way:

All men by nature are qualified to see certain thresholds of
truth as they are revealed by God in the facts of nature, but it
takes a special gift from God to have faith in the Bible as truth.
Yet, when the Christian, to whom this gift is given, is called
upon to give an account of his faith, and when he is warned,
"Beloved, do not believe every spirit, false prophets have gone
out into the world" (1 John 4:1), he is not lost for a test by

which to learn whether his faith is properly grounded or not. This test is systematic consistency. If what is being believed makes peace with the law of contradiction and the facts of experience, it is a faith which is prompted by the Spirit of God. If what is being believed fails to correspond with the mind of God, i.e., is not systematically consistent, such a faith is prompted by other than the Spirit of God. The Spirit can speak only the truth; it can witness only the mind of God.[7]

A Personal Note

Let me summarize these deliberations about religious epistemology by an example of what this all looks like in practice. The limitations of the present inquiry will not let me carry this out in detail, but I can at least give a programmatic outline. The illustration will be personal. I am a Christian. What might the thinking of a person who is committed both to philosophical criticism and to Christianity look like? To begin with, the autobiographical details of my conversion to Christianity need not detain us, though once I was committed to the Christian belief system I came to regard the events which led to my conversion as significant and purposive. Christianity makes sense out of my personal and intellectual existence. The last sentence is my thinking in a nutshell, but obviously it requires some elaboration.

By now it should be clear what it would mean for Christianity to make sense out of one's intellectual existence. The internal structure of the Christian belief system has as its key interpretive concepts a God who is complexly personal and who is Creator and Sustainer of the natural order; finite persons who are created with a need for a relation to God, but who act and value and choose within the natural order in a way that has estranged them from God; and the entrance of God into the historical process in the person of Jesus Christ to effect through his death and resurrection a restoration of finite persons to himself.[8]

The internal structure which is an elaboration of these key concepts must be consistent and coherent. This means that I must face, squarely and without hedging, allegations that this view of God is inconsistent with my beliefs about the presence of evil in the world; or that the theological doctrine of the Trinity is internally inconsistent; or that there are inconsistencies between my beliefs about God's overruling providence and human freedom of action. I must also be willing to face squarely all available data which has any bearing on the truth-value of my beliefs. This means that I must test the Christian accounts of events surrounding God's redemptive activity in history against reasonable interpretations of ancient records and archeological findings; I must show how a Christian understanding of humanity and nature can incorporate scientific data about these areas (always sensitive to the limitations of empirical inquiry and the way in which the personal interpretive schemes of the scientists may influence the way they regard the significance of the data); and I must be willing to extend my Christian interpretive scheme without hesitation into every area of human experience, showing how it relates to literary experience, present historical processes and human culture in the largest sense, to mention just a few examples.[9] All of this still leaves out the one area which on a day-to-day basis concerns each of us more than all of the others— personal experience.

Part of the data with which my interpretive scheme must be able to deal is the complex of joys, satisfactions, minor irritations and major tragedies that makes up my lived experience. What is *my* life all about? Clearly an interpretive scheme that is capable of uniting broader theoretical adequacy with answers to questions of personal existence will be exceedingly powerful. As a Christian I claim that Christianity does exactly that. My belief that Christianity is true permits me to enter into the process of criticism with enthusiasm and without reservation. The momentous nature of Christianity's claims makes it crucial that I throw myself into the testing process with honesty and full integrity. After all,

what could be more important than discovering whether such a
scheme has the marks of falsity or the marks of truth? It is only
in the epistemological arena, thus broadly conceived, that such an
issue can be pursued for Christianity or any other world view.

Notes

Chapter 1: Introductory Considerations

[1]Bertrand Russell, *The Problems of Philosophy* (New York: Oxford Univ. Press, 1912), p. 17.

[2]This wave of literature began with an article by Edmund L. Gettier, "Is Justified True Belief Knowledge?" *Analysis* 23 (1963), pp. 121-23. Worthwhile and accessible discussions of this problem may also be found in Michael Williams, *Groundless Belief* (New Haven, Conn.: Yale Univ. Press, 1977), pp. 5-12; Stephen T. Davis, *Faith, Skepticism and Evidence* (Lewisburg, Pa.: Bucknell Univ. Press, 1978), pp. 32-37; and Anthony Quinton, "Knowledge and Belief," in *The Encyclopedia of Philosophy*, 8 vols., ed. Paul Edwards (New York: Macmillan, 1967), 4:345ff.

[3]John L. Pollock, *Knowledge and Justification* (Princeton: Princeton Univ. Press, 1974), p. 7. A number of helpful remarks relevant to these introductory considerations are found in Nicholas Wolterstorff, "Justified Belief" (unpublished paper).

[4]Plato *Meno* 97D and following.

[5]As is done by Peter Unger in *Ignorance: A Case for Skepticism* (Oxford: Clarendon Press, 1975). See remarks by Williams in *Groundless Belief*, pp. 7ff.

[6]I am indebted to Keith Cooper for suggesting this distinction.

Chapter 2: Approaches to Justification

[1]The argument which follows is drawn from Descartes' *Meditations on First Philosophy*. A helpful account of Descartes' philosophy by Bernard Williams may be found in *The Encyclopedia of Philosophy*, 2:344-54.

[2]See D. W. Hamlyn, "A Priori and A Posteriori," and Bernard Williams, "Rationalism," in *The Encyclopedia of Philosophy*, ed. Paul Edwards, 1:140-44 and 7:69-75; "Necessary Truth," in Monroe C. Beardsley and Elizabeth Lane Beardsley, *Philosophical Thinking: An Introduction* (New York: Harcourt, Brace and World, 1965), pp. 242-48, and Arthur F. Holmes, *Faith Seeks Understanding* (Grand Rapids, Mich.: Eerdmans, 1971), pp. 37ff.

[3]Frederick Ferré, *Basic Modern Philosophy of Religion* (New York: Scribner's, 1967), p. 143.

[4]See T. E. Hill, *Contemporary Theories of Knowledge* (New York: Ronald Press, 1961), pp. 79-124; Jean-Paul Sartre, *Being and Nothingness*, trans. Hazel E. Barnes (New York: Philosophical Library, 1956), pt. 3, chap. 1, sect. 4; Henri Bergson, *An Introduction to Metaphysics*, trans. T. E. Hulme (New York: Putnam's, 1912); Frederick Ferré, *Language, Logic and God* (New York: Harper & Row, 1961), chaps. 7 and 8.

[5]Merle B. Turner, *Philosophy and the Science of Behavior* (New York: Appleton-Century-Crofts, 1967), pp. 191-92.

[6]See Bacon's *Novum Organum* and Mill's "A System of Logic," in *John Stuart Mill's Philosophy of Scientific Method*, ed. Ernest Nagel (New York: Hafner Publishing, 1950), esp. book 3.

[7]An excellent criticism of induction as a scientific method may be found in Carl G. Hempel, *Philosophy of Natural Science* (Englewood Cliffs, N.J.: Prentice-Hall, 1966), pp. 11ff.

[8]This was Descartes' view; see also Hill, *Contemporary Theories of Knowledge*, pp. 125-60.

[9]Bertrand Russell has a brilliant formulation of this approach in *Human Knowledge: Its Scope and Limits* (London: George Allen & Unwin, 1948), pt. 6, chap. 8; rpt. in Ernest Nagel and Richard Brandt, *Meaning and Knowledge: Systematic Readings in Epistemology* (New York: Harcourt, Brace and World, 1965), pp. 634-37. The Nagel and Brandt volume is an excellent source of illustrative material for many of the positions discussed in this book.

[10]The classical statement of this argument is in William Paley's *Natural Theology* (1802), now available as *Natural Theology: Selections*, ed. Frederick Ferré (Indianapolis: Bobbs-Merrill, 1963).

[11]For example, A. J. Ayer defended this view in *The Foundations of Empirical Knowledge* (New York: St. Martin's Press, 1947), chap. 5; rpt. in Nagel and Brandt, *Meaning and Knowledge*, pp. 570-76.

[12]David Hume, *Dialogues Concerning Natural Religion.* See Philo's argument at the end of pt. 2.

[13]For an elaboration of this point see the discussion of relevance in Irving M. Copi, *Introduction to Logic,* 5th ed. (New York: Macmillan, 1978), pp. 388-89.

[14]See Carl G. Hempel, *Philosophy of Natural Science,* pp. 10-18.

[15]Ibid., p. 16.

[16]Ibid., pp. 33-46.

[17]David Elton Trueblood, *Philosophy of Religion* (New York: Harper & Brothers, 1957), pp. 74-89; Cf. Edward John Carnell, *An Introduction to Christian Apologetics* (Grand Rapids, Mich.: Eerdmans, 1956), pp. 89-121; and Clark H. Pinnock, *Reason Enough* (Downers Grove, Ill.: InterVarsity Press, 1980).

[18]Carnell, *Christian Apologetics,* pp. 56-62.

[19]Cf. Hempel, *Philosophy of Natural Science,* p. 7; Trueblood, *Philosophy of Religion,* pp. 63-64.

[20]In the foregoing criticism of verification, I am clearly in debt to the writings of Sir Karl Popper. See especially his *Conjectures and Refutations* (New York: Harper & Row, 1968), pp. 33-59.

[21]See Norwood Russell Hanson, *Patterns of Discovery* (London: Cambridge Univ. Press, 1965), pp. 4-30.

[22]The classic account of this is Thomas S. Kuhn, *The Structure of Scientific Revolutions,* 2nd ed. (Chicago: Univ. of Chicago Press, 1970).

[23]Ibid., pp. 144-59.

[24]Kuhn's position is radicalized by Paul K. Feyerabend. See his "How to be a Good Empiricist—A Plea for Tolerance in Matters Epistemological," in *Philosophy of Science: The Delaware Seminar,* vol. 2, ed. Bernard Baumrin (New York: Interscience Publishers, 1963), pp. 3-39; and "Against Method: Outline of an Anarchistic Theory of Knowledge," in *Minnesota Studies in Philosophy of Science,* vol. 4, ed. Michael and Stephen Winokur (Minneapolis, Minn.: Univ. of Minnesota Press, 1970). See also the chapter entitled "Philosophical Agnosticism," in Milton K. Munitz, *The Mystery of Existence* (New York: Appleton-Century-Crofts, 1965).

[25]See John Hick, *Philosophy of Religion,* 2nd ed. (Englewood Cliffs, N.J.: Prentice-Hall, 1973), pp. 60-67, 87-96.

Chapter 3: The Problem of Criteria

[1]See his *From a Logical Point of View,* 2nd ed., rev. (New York: Harper & Row, 1961), pp. 42-44.

[2]See Frederick Ferré, *Basic Modern Philosophy of Religion* (New York: Scribner's, 1967), pp. 388-96.

[3]Ibid., p. 391.

[4]This expression is used by Keith E. Yandell in his *Basic Issues in the Philosophy*

of Religion (Boston: Allyn and Bacon, 1971), pp. 218ff.

[5]Ferré, *Philosophy of Religion,* p. 392.

[6]Nicholas Wolterstorff, *Reason within the Bounds of Religion* (Grand Rapids, Mich.: Eerdmans, 1976), pp. 62-63.

[7]Arthur F. Holmes, *Christian Philosophy in the Twentieth Century* (Nutley, N.J.: Craig Press, 1969), p. 234. Holmes's discussion on pp. 232ff. is very worthwhile.

[8]Quine, *From a Logical Point of View,* p. 41.

[9]See Wolterstorff, *Reason within Bounds,* pp. 24ff. and M. Williams, *Groundless Belief.*

[10]In some philosophical literature the words *ontology* (adjective: ontological) and *metaphysics* are used interchangeably. I have tried to use *ontology* to refer to views about the kinds of things that exist, while reserving *metaphysical* for elaborate views which spell out the relations of these things and the structure of reality generally. On this use the view that there are both physical and spiritual substances would be ontological. The view that human beings are composites of these two substances but that animals are only physical (Descartes' view) would be metaphysical.

[11]A good bit of ink has been spilled on questions of the nature of truth and theory of reference in recent philosophical literature. Most of the time the disputants fail to make logical contact with each other because they fail to see that their respective interpretive frameworks determine their answers to these issues. The result is that each produces arguments which make sense from inside his scheme, but no internal criticism of the other's view is produced. For an example of this see the exchange between Richard Rorty and Bruce Aune in *The Journal of Philosophy* 69 (1972): 649-67.

[12]Even the logical atomists, who thought of reality as a collection of independent facts, were committed to the coherence criterion. The judgment "nothing is related to anything else" *does* specify what relations obtain in reality, though it is entirely negative. An adequate map may indeed show you that you cannot get there from here. Commitment to conceptual interrelatedness does not entail that you believe reality to be an interrelated whole (unless you also believe that reality *is* that conceptual system, as some idealists did).

[13]"Consolations for the Specialist," in *Criticism and the Growth of Knowledge,* ed. Imre Lakatos and Alan Musgrave (London: Cambridge Univ. Press, 1970), p. 226.

[14]Of course this is not a psychological claim. One might have an experience which would be crucial for one's whole life. Experiences of conversion (religious, political and even scientific) are examples of this. A reader of this book in earlier manuscript form aptly comments, "Could it be that in conversion

the web [of beliefs] is changed not by a series of attacks from the edges but by a profound destruction of the center? Of course . . . the ultimate rational warrant is the test of the new system which the conversion produces for the whole experience, but . . . particular episodes and experiences might still retain a decisive importance."

[15]*Physicalism* is the doctrine that all scientific statements must be formulated in a language consisting entirely of expressions about physical things and physical processes. Physics is the paradigm science in this view. The application of this view to the social sciences is behaviorism. Taken as an ontology, physicalism is a form of philosophical materialism.

[16]Paul K. Feyerabend has put considerable emphasis on the importance of pluralism for the testing of rival theories. Perhaps his most intelligible statement is "Outline of a Pluralistic Theory of Knowledge and Action," in *Planning for Diversity and Choice*, ed. Stanford Anderson (Cambridge, Mass.: MIT Press, 1968).

[17]*Corroborated* is used by Popper to speak of scientific theories which have withstood strong testing. Clearly, I have extended his use in applying it to interpretive schemes of unlimited scope.

[18]Criticisms which may legitimately be disregarded are considered in the discussion of doubt in chapter four.

[19]Keith Yandell, *Basic Issues in the Philosophy of Religion* (Boston: Allyn and Bacon, 1971), pp. 221-26, has an excellent discussion of the application of the criterion of consistency to interpretive schemes. See also my article, "The Behavior of Knowing: The Consequences of B. F. Skinner's Epistemology," *The Personalist* 56, no. 3 (summer 1975): 233-41, for an example of this criterion at work.

Chapter 4: Reason and Religious Belief

[1]Popper, *Conjectures and Refutations*, chap. 1.

[2]See Alvin Plantinga, "Is Belief in God Properly Basic?" *Nous* 15 (1981): 41-51.

[3]I am indebted to David M. Holley for calling attention to the word *discernment* in his unpublished paper "Faith and Evidence."

[4]An important study of the relation of social support to the maintenance of world views is Peter L. Berger and Thomas Luckmann, *The Sacred Canopy: Elements of a Sociological Theory of Religion* (New York: Doubleday, 1967).

[5]Very helpful in this regard is Os Guinness, *In Two Minds: The Dilemma of Doubt and How to Resolve It* (Downers Grove, Ill.: InterVarsity Press, 1976).

[6]There is a beautiful essay on this theme by Alfred Schutz entitled "Tiresias, or Our Knowledge of Future Events," in *Collected Papers*, vol. 2 (The Hague: Martinus Nijhoff, 1964), pp. 277-93.

[7]Carnell, *Christian Apologetics*, p. 70.

[8]See James W. Sire, *The Universe Next Door* (Downers Grove, Ill.: InterVarsity Press, 1976), chap. 2, for an outline of the basic beliefs of Christian theism.
[9]Though written from a verificationist point of view, Clark Pinnock's *Reason Enough* (Downers Grove, Ill.: InterVarsity Press, 1980) is a helpful orientation to a broad range of data from a Christian perspective.

Further Reading

The following list is intended as an answer to the question, "Where do I go from here?" It does not aim for scholarly completeness and is arguably idiosyncratic. The footnotes and bibliographies of these books will offset the self-imposed limitations of the present list.

On epistemology in general
Holmes, Arthur F. *Faith Seeks Understanding: A Christian Approach to Knowledge*. Grand Rapids, Mich.: Eerdmans, 1971.
Morton, Adam. *A Guide through the Theory of Knowledge*. Encino, Calif.: Dickenson Publishing, 1977.

On foundationalism and its problems
Morick, Harold, ed. *Challenges to Empiricism*. Belmont, Calif.: Wadsworth Publishing, 1972.
Williams, Michael. *Groundless Belief*. New Haven, Conn.: Yale Univ. Press, 1977.
Wolterstorff, Nicholas. *Reason within the Bounds of Religion*. Grand Rapids, Mich.: Eerdmans, 1976.

On relativism
Trigg, Roger. *Reason and Commitment*. London: Cambridge Univ. Press, 1973.

On rationality
Holmes, Arthur F. *Christian Philosophy in the Twentieth Century: An Essay in*

Philosophical Methodology. Nutley, N.J.: Craig Press, 1969.
Kekes, John. *A Justification of Rationality.* Albany: State Univ. of New York Press, 1976.

On religious knowledge (and related issues)
Ferré, Frederick. *Basic Modern Philosophy of Religion.* New York: Scribner's, 1967.
Gill, Jerry H. *On Knowing God.* Philadelphia: Westminster Press, 1981.
Yandell, Keith E. *Basic Issues in the Philosophy of Religion.* Boston: Allyn and Bacon, 1971.

On religious language
Dilley, Frank B. *Metaphysics and Religious Language.* New York: Columbia Univ. Press, 1964.
Ferré, Frederick. *Language, Logic, and God.* New York: Harper & Row, 1961.

On subjective and personal factors in religious belief
Davis, Stephen T. *Faith, Skepticism and Evidence: An Essay in Religious Epistemology.* Lewisburg, Pa.: Bucknell Univ. Press, 1978.
Evans, C. Stephen. *Subjectivity and Religious Belief: An Historical, Critical Study.* Grand Rapids, Mich.: Christian Univ. Press, 1978.
Mavrodes, George. *Belief in God: A Study in the Epistemology of Religion.* New York: Random House, 1970.

On the diversity of world views
Pepper, Stephen C. *World Hypotheses: A Study in Evidence.* Berkeley: Univ. of California Press, 1966.
Sire, James W. *The Universe Next Door: A Basic World View Catalog.* Downers Grove, Ill.: InterVarsity Press, 1976.